Speaking Out for Women ~
A Biblical View

Philip Siddons

Speaking Out for Women – A Biblical View

Judson Press ® Valley Forge

Speaking Out for Women—A Biblical View

Copyright © 1980
Judson Press, Valley Forge, PA 19481

Unless otherwise indicated, Bible quotations in this volume are from the Revised Standard Version of the Bible, copyrighted 1946, 1952, 1971, 1973 © by the Division of Christian Education of the National Council of the Churches of Christ in the United States of America, and are used by permission.

Other quotations of the Bible are from *The Jerusalem Bible,* copyright © 1966 by Darton, Longman & Todd, Ltd. and Doubleday and Company, Inc. Used by permission of the publisher.

Quotations from James Donaldson, *Woman: Her Position and Influence in Ancient Greece and Rome, and Among the Early Christians* (New York: Gordon Press, 1973) are used by permission of the publisher.

Library of Congress Cataloging in Publication Data

Siddons, Philip.
    Speaking out for women, a Biblical view.

    Bibliography: p.
    1.   Women (Christian theology)—Biblical teaching.
I.   Title.
BS680.W7S56   261.8'344   80-24007
ISBN 0-8170-0885-3

The name JUDSON PRESS is registered as a trademark in the U.S. Patent Office. Printed in the U.S.A. ⊕

To Linda,
who has taught me to dance
to the Creator's joyful tune
called life

Acknowledg- ments

I am most grateful for the support and patience of my wife, Linda, during this project. David M. Scholer was the first to introduce me to the positive direction of the Scriptures on the issue discussed in this book. I am very much in his debt for his disciplined bibliographies. I am also grateful to Nancy Ellis Leskiw, Paul Hammer, Dixis Lee Baker, and James Ashbrook for helping me in my research and writing.

Contents

Preface

A Story

"We've argued about this long enough. We'll do it my way; I'm the head of the house!" And with that as his final argument, forty-five-year-old Robert Moyer stormed out of the house and off to work.

Judy flopped down on the couch and tried to convince herself that she was used to this kind of attitude and behavior. "This is the way all couples act," she tried to tell herself. "If twenty-five years of marriage have accomplished anything, they have at least taught us to fight without raising our voices or using abusive language. After all," Judy considered, "we *are* Christians, but . . ."

Through her years of church affiliation, Judy had heard that a husband is to have the last say. Only rarely was the verse about a husband loving his wife "as Christ loved the church and gave himself up for her" (Ephesians 5:25) brought up in this context. That verse usually was used to indicate that husbands should remember their wives with Valentine's Day and anniversary gifts. "But isn't there more to it than that?" Judy wondered.

Judy knew that husbands had not been appointed head of the house by virtue of their superior intelligence or greater emotional stability. She thought back to the time Bob had argued that women should find fulfillment only in the home. He had said that the emotional makeup of women kept them from handling the pressures and responsibilities out in the "real world," as he put it. She laughed to herself because it had been Bob who had walked out of the conversation and slammed the door.

Judy got up from the couch, opened the front door to the quiet street, and yelled, "Life is real on both sides of this door!" She closed the door gently.

Judy knew that their argument was not the real issue. What was at stake was not a family decision; it had something to do with her personhood, her dignity, and her worth as a woman—a Christian woman, a married woman.

As Robert drove to work, he, too, was aware that the subject of their argument was unimportant. "But someone has to have the final say," he mumbled to himself as he drove slowly through the rush-hour traffic. To Robert, running a family was like controlling a city's traffic flow. Someone had to take the leadership and work the lights, or there would be accidents. But in the back of his mind lurked the realization that something was wrong with his neat and tidy view of human relationships.

"Where do you draw lines with this 'loving your wife like Christ loved the church'?" he asked himself. "No matter what Ephesians says," he continued to think, "the Bible still says something about women keeping silent and not teaching men."

And in recalling those teachings, Robert remembered a joke he had heard about women not being in heaven because of something in Revelation about silence. But Robert didn't laugh. Inside he wondered if he had missed something, if Christianity didn't have more to say about marriage and male-female relationships in general. "Maybe I'm afraid to find out," Robert thought to himself as he pulled into his reserved parking place just outside his office.

The Issue

As a minister, I have found in marriage and family counseling that many people have encountered similar experiences. Many Christians have begun to question prepackaged answers to human relationships. Men are becoming increasingly uncomfortable with traditional "male" molds. And women have led the way in questioning the apparent inconsistencies of the usual patterns of female-male relationships.

Unfortunately, many church leaders have selected passages of Scripture pertaining to women as the basis for doctrine or practice while completely ignoring the context of the passage and the directions of Scripture as a whole. In this book we will examine the key passages pertaining to women in light of their first-century context and historical background. We will follow a basic order of study, beginning by summarizing what life was like for women, first in ancient cultures and then in Hellenistic Greece and Rome. This is important because these nations influenced the status of women in Judaism. Next we will compare the place of women in Judaism with the customs of these non-Jewish cultures. In light of this, we will examine the Gospel writers' witness to how Jesus treated women and what the Acts of the Apostles and some of the New Testament epistles say about women in the early church. Finally, we will examine the relevance of these teachings for today's church and society.

Introduction

In examining any topic that the Bible addresses, it is always important to keep in mind that God deals with people through history, speaking to them in light of their particular situations. As students of the Bible, it is our responsibility to notice the general intent, as well as the specifics of these various witnesses to God's saving work through history. Whenever Christians look to the Bible for insight into particular concerns, such as the women's issue, it is necessary to establish *how* we understand and interpret the Bible, even before we begin to deal with its content.

First, from exploring the New Testament, we discover that it is a witness to the revelation of God in Jesus Christ. We consider the original writings of the New Testament authors to be witnesses to him, giving us varying proclamations of the foundational events of the Christian revelation. They tell us who Jesus was for them and how he was understood by the early church. Secondly, the Bible serves as a basis of faith and as a guide for the interpretation of faith. Because the Bible is considered as canon, a "measuring stick," regarding these matters, it is affirmed as the highest written authority for matters pertaining to our faith and the working out of our faith in our life-style.

The Bible witnesses to God's dealings with people through history.

Like a symphony, the Bible has contrasting themes, varying tones, and yet overwhelming harmonies. Studying the Bible, then, is similar to studying a person. We can never exhaustively explore all the depths; yet generalizations can be made as to its character.

Although we affirm that the biblical materials have present relevance, we also realize that the original writings were intended to communicate to people living in a culture two to three thousand years removed from ours. While the *synoptic* (i.e., "viewed together") Gospels (Matthew, Mark, and Luke) serve as our major witness to Jesus' deeds and teachings, we do not have direct access to them. It would be a mistake to think of the Gospels as some sort of videotape rerun of historical events. The witness to Jesus first took the form of stories which were told and retold, shaped and reshaped by followers of Jesus. Oral traditions about Jesus apparently were not committed to writing (in the form we now have it) until several decades after Jesus' death and resurrection. When these traditions were written down, the writers arranged the structure and content of their work to speak to the issues which touched on the life situations of the congregations they were addressing. It is our first task, then, to seek to understand passages in the New Testament in the settings of those who first read it. To do so, there are three concerns we need to consider to arrive at a fair meaning of any text.

Literary Concerns

First, we need to ask ourselves not only *what* the writer is talking about, but also *how* the subject is being discussed. This means that we examine the word meanings and grammatical analysis. It means that we study the sentence, the paragraph, and the chapter. It means that we investigate how the topic is discussed elsewhere in the author's writing and how the subject is addressed throughout the Bible. This involves the use of concordances and Bible dictionaries in our study.

When we read the Bible, we need to avoid interpreting passages in ways that were originally unintended. For example, we recognize that there are figures of speech in Scripture. "Trees clapping their hands" (see Isaiah 55:12) and "when the sun rises" (Psalm 104:22) we recognize as not literal statements. Rather, they are simply a kind of visual description in common language. We also look for variances in writing style, e.g., poetry, prose. Above all, as regards the New Testament writings, we recognize that first-century ways of saying things are not necessarily identical with our contemporary way of speaking.

Historical Concerns

To understand the Bible, we also need to pay attention to historical concerns. First-century Jewish culture was quite different from our twentieth-century Western culture. After all, Jesus did not use taxicabs and skyscrapers in his parables. Even more important, the social and economic experiences of first-century Judaism were vastly different from those of today. Although people's basic needs probably have remained constant through history, everyday experiences have changed drastically in the past two thousand years.

Questions about first-century religious and political practices need to be raised in order to understand the influences operating on believers then. It is particularly important to compare Jesus' teachings and actions with what we know of other teachings and customs of his times. In short, we cannot rob the biblical characters of their place in history. Jesus lived in a specific Jewish society, at a particular time in history, in the midst of a particular political, cultural, and religious life. It is, therefore, our responsibility first to see what was being said to people in the contexts of the first century and *then* to ask about applying it to our circumstances today.

Theological Concerns

We arrive at an author's theological understanding first by striving to understand what the Scriptures are saying in their contexts. By comparing what the writer says in one place with what he says in other places, we often gain additional insights into an author's theology. In this way, we avoid ascribing a theological position to an author based only on an isolated fragment of the author's entire work.

When studying New Testament passages, we recognize that all writings were intended for specific church contexts. It is useful, however, to attempt to distinguish a statement of practical and specific advice to an individual or group for one of broader theological affirmation. For instance, there is a difference between the advice for men to pray "lifting holy hands" (1 Timothy 2:8) or to "greet one another with a holy kiss" (1 Corinthians 16:20) and the statement "if you confess with your lips that Jesus is Lord and believe in your heart that God raised him from the dead, you will be saved" (Romans 10:9). In the first two instances the advice pertained to specific acts. The passage from Romans gives a broader theological truth, albeit in a letter to a specific congregation. At times the attempt to make this distinction is difficult, particularly in cases where we have little or no information about the original readers' life situation which precipitated the writing.

We also understand that any given Scripture passage may never exhaust a subject, and on some subjects the Bible is silent. But the biblical witnesses do provide general guidelines for us as we grapple with issues that confront us now.

The Issue of Women in Church and Society

The impact of the women's movement has caused many to reexamine their ideas about women in our culture. It has caused Christians everywhere to think differently about women in church and society.

Until the Industrial Revolution late in the last century society had been dependent on the physical strength required in manual labor. While some women were involved in heavy farming tasks prior to this time, women were generally relegated to the home, while men dominated the working world. It was rare to see a woman in leadership in the business world, whether in an office or a plant. The need, however, for physical strength, particularly in industry, largely has been met by technological improvements. There have been many changes in career opportunities for women, and the role expectancies for women have become considerably more diversified. Women today have vocational responsibilities that were formerly held by men only. Many of the old taboos prohibiting women from working outside of the home have disappeared. For instance, there is a woman in charge of an oil drilling rig off the coast of our country. There also are women in steel plants, operating cranes, and working in other positions that long have been sought after by men with seniority.

Another factor in the changing role of women in our society is education. In this century there has been a dramatic change in educational opportunities for achievements by women. In the United States there is an almost universal equality for women in terms of higher educational options, particularly since World War II.[1] The old myths that say women are intellectually inferior are considered poor jokes at best. Hundreds of books are being published each year by and for women. Not only are textbook writers making their language inclusive of women, but also entire fields are opening up in women's studies. Psychology, sociology, religion, art, and business majors in colleges are including courses specifically designed to meet the needs of women in today's society.

As greater numbers of women assume positions of leadership in society, people are discovering how antiquated and oppressive certain traditions have been for women. Christians now look for answers to the question of where the women's movement needs to go. The church has been addressing this subject, but there is confusion. Some reject outright the so-called "problem passages" of the New Testament. Others have retreated in frustration to the convenience of their lifelong beliefs. Unfortunately, even greater numbers have given up dealing with the issue. They have decided to wait until the culture at large decides for them.

By the late seventies, most major Protestant denominations had elevated women to leadership positions in the church. Yet more traditional-minded churches still hesitate to accept the leadership of women. There are hundreds of churches that deny women leadership roles, whether as ministers, elders, or deacons. In view of their understanding of New Testament passages that appear to prohibit it, many in our churches feel reluctant to permit women's leadership.

But with the growing opportunities for women in most parts of society, many Christians are being forced to reconsider their biblical interpretations. The options appear to be this: if the Bible prohibits women's leadership and equality, then the egalitarianism in our society must be against Christianity. On the other hand, if the changes in society seem to be right for human relationships, then one must reevaluate his or her interpretation of various biblical passages. This is the tension many in the pew are facing. But there is the danger of trying to make Scripture conform to one's experience. This need not be the case. If we examine the whole of Scripture, along with the passages relevant to the women's issues, we may arrive at fresh biblical understandings about how we view such issues.

The church is called to speak to issues related to marriage, the family, child rearing, and being single. People are demanding a clear and decisive word about relationships between men and women. The struggle to pass the Equal Rights Amendment has reminded us that the women's movement has had a profound social impact in our country.

As Christians speak to the issue, they need to be prepared to address not only the question of how women and men relate in the church but also in other areas. We need to be able to apply what Christianity says about women and men to literature, the media, art, music, and all other aspects of life. For how women and men respond to one another affects the homemaker, the business person, the gas station attendant, the president, the laundromat attendant, the minister, and the worker on the assembly line. What has become known as the "women's issue" is a most important issue because it affects everyone who lives on the earth.

As a minister I have opportunities to share in many happy relationships. I have seen the nervous but marvelously joyful faces of young couples repeating their wedding vows. When baptizing children and praying for God's guidance of their parents, I often have become overcome with a sense of awe, hardly able to complete the prayer.

But I have seen brokenness in relationships as well. I have seen parents sadly watch their son go to jail because of his irresponsibility. I have seen individuals live out their lives feeling worthless. I have sat with sobbing people who were waiting for the bodies of their husbands and wives to be taken away. But some of the most severe and hopeless problems I have seen have resulted from the domination of men over women.

It is one thing to have the person closest to you die. It may be worse to have a person treat you all your life as if you are less than an equal. Many women suffer intense oppression because they are sharing their lives with husbands who view them on a lower level and treat them with a standard different from their own. Women are often excluded from, or are limited in, decision making in and outside of the home.

There are women who are ordered around the house by their husbands as if they were slaves. Surprisingly, there are Christian husbands with so low a view of women that it is unthinkable for them to let their wives know about or have access to the money they earn. "After all," they reason, "it's my money, I earn it." Because of the male domination in our society that has existed through the centuries, there are an astounding number of people who believe that women are in some ways unequal to men. It is to these conflicts that the church must now speak.

STUDY QUESTIONS FOR CHAPTER 1

1. We see change in the role of women in our society. List some of the changes you have experienced, and explain why you think they came about.

2. Your own denomination may have adopted changes in its understanding of women in the church, or it may have maintained a traditional stance. What is its stand, and what is the reasoning for its position?

3. Reread the short story in the Preface of the book. What are the conflicts and the issues involved in this situation?

4. As Christians we often face differing interpretations of biblical passages. In the event that two equally sincere groups of Christians disagree on a biblical issue, how can they study the problem together?

5. Do you feel that the principles for studying Scripture that are outlined in the Introduction (studying the literary, historical, and theological concerns of Scripture passages) are being used in your congregation's teaching situations?

Women in Pagan Cultures

Chapter 2

The history of the Jewish people is replete with evidence of how God relates to humanity. Christians, as well as Jews, can discover much about God's dealings with people by a study of Jewish customs and traditions. However, the Jews throughout their history never have been totally isolated from their surrounding and sometimes governing nations. The customs and traditions of bordering countries have frequently influenced them, as can be seen by the repeated condemnations of Israel by the Old Testament prophets for duplicating the sins of its neighbors.

Archaeological studies have shown that the prominent deities of ancient Sumer, Babylon, and Egypt were female.[1] In Merlin Stone's impressive work, she argues that cultures preceding the Hebrew peoples by thousands of years worshiped Ashtoreth (or Astarte).[2] The existence of the worship of female deities continued until about 500 C.E. when Christian emperors of Rome and Byzantium closed down the few remaining temples. According to Stone, worship of the female deity was widespread throughout the ancient world, and in some cultures women were considered superior politically and socially to the men. For instance, in Libya and Ethiopia fifty years before Christ, all authority supposedly was vested in women.[3]

A gradual change to a predominance of male deities occurred in the Middle East, however, as Indo-Europeans conquered the lands between 2400 and 1000 B.C.E. As the male deities gained supremacy, the divine right to thrones, which formerly went to women, was eventually shifted to men.[4]

During biblical times, as it had been for thousands of years before in Sumer, Babylon, and Canaan, temple worship frequently involved women living in the temple complex, having sex with the area's men out of reverence for the goddess.[5] But reverence of the female deity was gradually destroyed by the Indo-European invaders and later by the Hebrews, as well as by the Greeks, the Romans, and the Christians.

Women in Greek Societies

In the classical Greek world prior to the Hellenistic period,[6] women had a considerably lower place in society than men. Judging by the epic literature, law codes, public records, and art of the Greeks, women were thought to be fickle, inferior in all ways to men, and highly susceptible to immorality and foreign cultic practices.[7] In classical Greek societies, women were considered by men to be things, not persons. Although the goddess Aphrodite and the goddess Athena were held in honor among the Greeks, throughout the early literature there is a pronounced bitterness against women in general.[8] This may have been a reaction to the higher position of women in earlier times.

Some Greek writers referred to women as the greatest evil that the gods ever created, a necessary evil, the specious curse to man. In Greek religions there was honor given to priestesses in certain religious cults, but women were deemed totally unfit to lead in any capacity, religious or otherwise. "A brainless woman is most of all to be desired, and a woman of keen wit most of all to be dreaded."[9]

The leading philosophers of the Greeks, Plato and Aristotle, taught that women should be given access to philosophy and education, but they also insisted that too much freedom for women would be detrimental. Women were to be subject to men.[10]

The assumption that women are intellectually and morally inferior to men pervades the early Greek law codes. Since a woman was valued only for propagation of the race and for satisfying the passions of a man, she was considered a man's property under the law. While the husband was permitted to have concubines, the wife was expected to be faithful. In keeping with the ancient Hammurabi law code, the Greeks permitted a husband to divorce his wife for any reason, but a wife could never obtain a divorce.[11]

During the Hellenistic and Roman periods which followed, the status of women changed dramatically. While most women were excluded from participation in government, there were some exceptions. The Hellenistic queens generally had considerable influence in political affairs because of their position in the courts. Cleopatra in 51 B.C.E. inherited the throne of Egypt with her brother, Ptolemy XIII. Olympias, the mother of Alexander the Great, presided over the Macedonian court in his absence; and Arsinoe, ruling with her brother Ptolemy II, was responsible for the expansion of Egyptian sea power.[12]

Legally, women in Greece had few rights. For instance, it was against the law for a woman alone to make any contracts. However, Hellenistic law was not uniform throughout the empire. For example, Greek women were always under a male guardian;[13] Egyptian women were not. The guardians would enable Greek women to control slaves, officially own land, and make contracts. Greek women could also purchase, sell, be lessors and lessees, borrow, and pay taxes.[14] Women in Egypt could petition the government; yet they were not permitted to write a contract. Apparently throughout the Hellenized nations, a father could dissolve his daughter's marriage, even against her will.[15]

In the Greek cultures, women citizens were generally not educated other than in domestic things. There is evidence from signatures discovered on Egyptian papyri, however, that some women had learned to read and write.[16] In Sparta, women mixed freely with men, and it was said that there women owned up to two-fifths of the land. Sappho stands out as one Spartan woman who was educated.[17] But this lifestyle for Spartan women seemed to be the exception. Greek women were to seek respectability in motherhood. A woman's place was generally limited to the home.

Historians show that Greek women of the higher classes lived in the "women's quarters" of the home. They ate meals with their husbands only if guests were not present. Respectable Greek women were discouraged from meeting men in public. Reasons for going out of the house were to participate in a festival, make purchases, or fulfill a religious duty. Even in these cases, however, the women were to be escorted by a male slave.[18]

Greek women in early Hellenistic times were kept mainly out of the public eye. They were frequently told that their chief duties were to stay in the home and obey their husbands.[19] With these limitations, one would think it nearly impossible for women to grow intellectually or culturally. Because marriages were arranged by parents, the relationship between a husband and wife tended to be a matter of duty and custom rather than a mutually satisfying relationship based on love. Some historians think that the status of women and limitations confining women probably militated against any attempt to make marriage a relationship of fellowship and mutual growth.[20]

If a wife spent most of her time within the home and was denied access to education and society, it would not be surprising if she were unable to participate in an informed and stimulating conversation with her husband. Greek men were known to go elsewhere for their conversations as well as for their sexual fulfillment, and adultery was prevalent in Greek societies. Prostitution was incorporated into the worship rituals at the Greek temples that men frequented. One temple to Aphrodite in Corinth was said to have had a thousand prostitutes in its employ.[21]

The most well-known Greek women were the *hetaerae* ("companions"), prostitutes who were educated so that they could give men the cultured and intellectual companionship that their wives could not provide.[22] As the Athenian Demosthenes said: "We have hetaerae for our pleasure, concubines for the daily needs of the body, and wives so we may have legitimate children and a faithful steward of our houses."[23]

Women in Roman Society

Under Roman rule,[24] many of the previous laws regarding women's status continued. At every age a woman was forced to live under the authority of a man, whether it was her father, brother, husband, adult son, or appointed male guardian. Roman women were not permitted to appear in courts.[25] First-century women were considered to be the property of their husbands under Roman law, and a Roman man had absolute authority over his wife.[26] If his wife were accused of a crime, he could punish her in any manner. A Roman could divorce his wife for infidelity, for stealing the keys to his wine, for going about with her face unveiled, or for going to the games without his permission.[27] A woman could not marry or sell property without the consent of her legal male guardian.[28] Male supremacy was so extensively imbedded in the law that limitations were even placed on how much a woman could inherit from her husband's estate.[29]

The only women legally free from their fathers were the vestal virgins who served in the various temples. Since women were limited in their participation in politics and society, religious cults, both national and imported oriental cults, attracted them.[30] In these popular cults, women would acquire leadership positions as priestesses, temple guardians, or cultic prostitutes. In the capital of Rome, vestal virgins figured prominently in all of the emperor's public festivities.

At the time the New Testament was written, women in Hellenistic societies were participating in religion more frequently than in previous times. Roman wives were in attendance with their husbands at the temple.

Socially, a first-century woman had to depend totally on her husband for her friends, her gods, and her cultural improvement. But there were advancements for women both inside and outside the home. Whereas Greek women lived in separate sections of their homes, Roman women in Christ's time were taking part in all activities of home life. A Roman woman was the mistress of the house and was in charge of the servants. She was responsible for the storehouses and often did the bookkeeping tasks.

A Roman woman was permitted access to her husband's public life as well. The Roman matron received her husband's friends, accompanied her husband to banquets and games, and at times went with him to the senate.[31]

Women of the lower classes worked in wealthier homes as spinners, weavers, clothes makers, wet nurses, child nurses, and cooks. Some even had special training as secretaries, maids, hairdressers, masseuses, readers, entertainers, and midwives. Some freedwomen making up the Roman working class were shopkeepers, artisans, waitresses, and prostitutes.[32]

Some of these improvements for women were a result of the teachings of the Roman Stoics. One Stoic philosopher, Musonius Rufus,[33] suggested that women should study religion and philosophy and have the same educational opportunities as men. He also recommended that women be permitted to work outside of the home. Marriage, according to Musonius, should be a relationship of companionship and mutual love.[34]

Like Musonius Rufus, Plutarch had many positive suggestions for the advancement of women.[35] He urged wives to be jovial and humorous with their husbands and not to worry about being considered too forward. He also suggested that marriage could be commonality of mind and urged women to use every means at their disposal to grow as persons.[36] While many negative attitudes about women were held throughout the Greco-Roman world, it would be a mistake to infer that all males were women haters. The point is that the cultures surrounding and governing the Jews were dominated by men with definite attitudes, teachings, laws, and customs that subordinated women to men. These societies considered women to be inferior to men and restricted them accordingly. These practices were observed by the Jews and probably affected their life-style as well.

STUDY QUESTIONS FOR CHAPTER 2

1. Since we are not under the domination of a foreign power, it is difficult for those who live in the United States to understand how one country influences the affairs of another. Look up: Deuteronomy 23:17-18; 1 Kings 14:24; 15:12; 22:46; Hosea 13:1-3. What practices from the surrounding countries had influenced the Jews to the extent that they became very much a part of the Jewish way of life?

2. What would it be like today if women were not permitted to own material possessions, to have credit, to acquire an education, and were considered to be the property of their fathers or husbands? What changes in your life would have to take place if this were the case today?

3. Even if women of those times knew no other way of life, do you suppose these rules and restrictions had a general effect on women as individuals? If you were a woman in those times, how would these things influence your thinking and growth as a person?

4. Much has changed for women since Greek and Roman times. Why have there been improvements for women since then?

5. It is certainly obvious that women in ancient times were conditioned to adjust to their culture's injustices. Today if oppressed individuals are willing to tolerate injustices, what is a Christian's responsibility in addressing an unjust situation?

Chapter 3

Women in Early Judaism

In reaction to the religious practices of the surrounding peoples, Israel condemned those who followed the customs of the neighboring pagans.[1] Stone interestingly suggests the possibility that the Levite priests were descendants of the conquering Indo-European Luvian peoples who were so opposed to the female deities in the societies they conquered.[2] Stone's thesis is that in a time when it was considered acceptable for women to prostitute themselves for a goddess, the Levite priests devised a concept of sexual morality for women with the long-range intention of maneuvering males into the power structure instead of females.[3] In other words, to switch over to a patriarchal system, the men would have to gain power of land ownership and have firm control of their male offspring in order to establish a patrilineal system.[4]

According to Stone, the Israelites attempted in several ways to downgrade the existing respect for Astarte, who was the principle deity of southern Canaan. They misspelled her name; they referred to her only in the masculine gender, and they consistently linked her name with her male consort. Reverence for the female deity stood in direct conflict with the religion of Israel. Condemnations for worshiping Baal and Ashtoreth are in Judges 2:13; 3:7; and 1 Samuel 7:3, 4. First Kings 15:13 tells of Queen Maacah being dethroned because of her worship of Asherah. Jeremiah 44:15-19 tells of an incident taking place around 600 B.C.E. in a Hebrew colony in Egypt where Israel adopted a new religion, offering incense to the queen of heaven. About 735-727 B.C.E. King Ahaz followed the ancient religion, and in 620 B.C.E. women of Ezekiel's time were involved in a practice directly linked with the female deity.[5]

There is little doubt, then, that the religion of the peoples surrounding Israel had great influence on the people, and those who formed and led the religion of Israel reacted strongly against it.

Since most of the information we have about women in first-century Judaism comes from the writings of a small number of rabbis,[6] we know little about the common beliefs and practices of the broad masses. The picture of women in rabbinic Judaism is only a reflection of the views of rabbis in second-century Judaism and onwards, and even then this picture is only a generalization, and we cannot assume that everyone adhered to these beliefs and practices without exception.[7]

Judaism as a religion and a culture was based on a patriarchy similar to that of classical Greece. The central unit in Jewish life was, and is today, the family. Men were the leaders not only of the family and religion but also of the government. Men maintained the leadership positions in all aspects of life. This was true not only in the early times of the patriarchs, such as Abraham, but also in first-century society. In comparison to our own time, in many families where grandparents have remained in the household the grandfather strongly influences the family decision-making process. It was a similar situation in Jewish households. But while the men held leadership roles in religion, government, and in the home, women occupied themselves with supportive tasks, especially in the home.[8]

Women in Jewish Religion

Women were segregated from men in the temple and synagogues.[9] In the Jerusalem temple built by Herod during the first century, women were permitted only in the "court of heathens" or "the women's court." The "women's court" was built just five steps above that of the "heathens" and fifteen steps below that of the men.[10]

The neighborhood synagogues had two parts, the lecture hall and the worship room. Women never went into the lecture hall and could be present in the worship room only if they remained behind a special screen. Both in the temple and the synagogues women entered through separate entrances. They were not allowed to read the Torah publicly nor to participate in worship except during the congregational prayers.[11]

While men studied, prayed, and worshiped daily, women maintained the household and did everything to enable the men to further their own religious instruction. In order to give women the time to maintain such a supportive atmosphere in the home, they were exempted from following all commandments and laws that mentioned time. That is, if there was a command to do something daily or weekly, such as pray or go to the synagogue, women were exempted from doing it. The general tendency of the Jewish laws shifted women's responsibilities to the home life, away from performing publicly in the synagogues or even in front of members of their own family.[12] In short, women were not encouraged to do things that would distract them from household duties. The only educational responsibility women had was to send their husbands and sons off to study. There were some rare exceptions, such as Beruria of the mid-second century and Imma Shalom. Both women had knowledge of the Law and were respected for it.[13] Some upper-class daughters learned Greek, but generally daughters were not even given private tutors because it was feared that the girl's father might be tempted sexually by the woman teaching his daughter.[14] Because of the supportive role women played, the men were free to study religion and run society.

Because of the differences between men's and women's roles, the rabbis were grateful that they were men and not women. It was certainly a greater privilege to learn and study the Torah than not, as evidenced by this prayer instruction: "A man is obliged to offer three benedictions daily: that he has made me an Israelite, that he has not made me a woman, that he has not made me a boor."[15]

Women in Jewish Law

For the entirety of a woman's life, she remained legally a minor. As in the Greek and Roman cultures, a woman in Judaism was always under the jurisdiction of either her father, husband, eldest son, or nearest male relative. She was considered the legal property of her husband.[16] In Jewish literature women were frequently grouped together with slaves, beasts, and property. Since women were considered to be the property of men, they received inheritances only when there were no sons.[17] Also, women were apparently not considered reliable enough to give evidence in a trial.[18] Women were disqualified from bearing

witness because of their supposed inferior minds.[19] Judicial actions
were initiated only by men.

Although marriage meant that a woman would become the property
of the man, there were high ideals set forth for the relationship.[20]

One safeguard to protect women in Judaism from being easily
divorced was the premarriage contract called the *Kethubah*. It involved
a financial agreement whereby the wife would receive a certain amount
of money in the event of divorce or her husband's death. Its origins
may have been in the older custom of the prospective husband paying
the father of his fiancée a sum of money that was set aside to care for
her in the event of his death.[21]

Jewish legislation regarding divorce is full of theological dispute,
however, and it is not at all clear that there was a universal code
followed. What emerges, though, is a seeming powerlessness for
women regarding divorce. Grounds for divorce were based on a
woman's having transgressed the Law of Moses or Jewish customs.
The grounds were based on commentaries on Deuteronomy 24:1-4,
which says that if a husband finds some "indecency" in his wife, he
could divorce her. Despite the complexity of Jewish divorce laws, a
man could generally divorce his wife for a variety of grounds and not
have to pay the Kethubah financial contract.[22] To protect women, there
were, however, restrictions on men divorcing their wives. If a man had
seduced a woman and was caught, he was forced to marry her by law
and could never divorce her (see Deuteronomy 22:28-29).[23] We do not
know what the "average" divorce proceeding was like for women at
the time of Jesus, but we would assume that women did not have as
much leverage as men in the matter.

A divorced woman was in a disadvantageous position since there
was no career for women other than marriage. Because of the legal,
social, educational, and economic restrictions on Jewish women, a
divorced woman's failure to find another husband to support her would
force her to rely on relatives for survival.

On the whole, women did not have power in the courts, but they
were judged on the same basis as a man when accused of crimes.[24] The
assumption that women were more corrupt than men can be seen in the
ritual test for adultery mentioned in Numbers 5:11-31. Only the woman
was forced to drink the dusty liquid and to stand before the crowd with
her nakedness exposed and with a rope around her neck. The man
never had to undergo this humiliating ritual.[25]

The idea of the moral inferiority of women was based on the

rabbis' interpretation of Genesis. They thought that because Eve sinned first, she was morally weaker than Adam and more susceptible to corruption.[26]

> "I will greatly multiply your pain in childbearing;
>   in pain you shall bring forth children,
> yet your desire shall be for your husband,
>   and *he shall rule over you*."
>   (Genesis 3:16, italics added)

The rabbis regarded this statement about male domination as a divine ordinance. That is, they taught that God *wanted* men to dominate women. The rabbis apparently did not hold the view that Genesis was *describing* part of the unfortunate and sorrowful outcome of sin coming into the world. Yet the rest of the curse was viewed as *descriptive* rather than *prescriptive*. In the same context God said that men would have difficulty earning a living (Genesis 3:17), that there would be a breakdown in nature's unity (Genesis 3:18), and, finally, that people would die (Genesis 3:19).

The rabbis interpreted the word *helper* (Genesis 2:18) to mean that women were made to be subordinate. When one person helps another, however, it doesn't indicate that the helper is inferior. Also, the rabbis apparently did not think that women were created in God's image. However, male and female are both included in the verse that says we are created in the image of God: ". . . in his . . . image . . . he created *them*" (Genesis 1:27, italics added).

Women in Jewish Society

The Jewish leaders observed the moral laxity of Greece and Rome. They saw how the education of pagan women brought them into closer contact with men. They seemed to judge the rising status of women in contemporary Rome to be a contributer to social evils. Therefore, Jewish women were given neither an education nor many social opportunities.

The writer Philo informs us that in Alexandria women were kept in the seclusion of the home.[27] When a guest would be entertained in a Jewish household, the unmarried daughters were to remain in the back rooms. Decent and upstanding Jewish women were not to go beyond the front door. In the country women were freer to go outside the home, but women who lived in the city generally lived in the "women's quarters."[28] This probably was not the custom throughout Palestine, for the New Testament describes a more open life-style for women. It was the custom, however, that if women went outside of the home, they were to wear veils over their faces. If they failed to do so, it was grounds for divorce.[29]

Ben Sirach, a scribe during the Hellenistic period when the Seleucids controlled the Jews, had strong views on women:

> No wickedness comes anywhere near the wickedness of a woman,
>   may a sinner's lot be hers!. . .
> Bad temper, insolence and shame hold sway
>   where the wife supports the husband. . . .
> Sin began with a woman,
>   and thanks to her we all must die.
>   (Ecclesiasticus 25:19, 22,24, *The Jerusalem Bible*)

Like other Old Testament writers, he seemed to express positive thoughts as well:

> Happy the husband of a really good wife;
>   the number of his days will be doubled.
> A perfect wife is the joy of her husband,
>   he will live out the years of his life in peace.
>   (Ecclesiasticus 26:1-2, *The Jerusalem Bible*)

Because of this apparent negativity toward women in Judaism, various superstitions arose in the culture. Genesis 1 describes women and men in God's image. Genesis 2 tells the story of Eve coming from Adam's rib. Therefore, to offset an attempt to understand men and women as equals, the myth of Lilith was created. In Jewish mythology, it was said that Adam's first wife (described in Genesis 1) was Lilith, who ruined the relationship because she considered herself equal to her husband.[30]

Some argue that the place of women in Judaism was actually higher than in pagan cultures. They point out that in the wisdom literature women are frequently treated positively.[31] Wisdom itself is used in the feminine gender. Proverbs 31 highly praises assertive and resourceful wives. The very fact that Miriam, Deborah, Hannah, Abigail, Huldah, and Esther were considered prophetesses shows that there was some consciousness of women as worthwhile people who could be leaders.[32] The fact remains, however, that except for the Song of Songs, where the focus is on the woman who initiates most of the action,[33] women were praised only when they were doing well at fitting into their prescribed roles: mothering, managing a home, or using their womanly sensuality in a courageous way.

Judging by the standards of today's Western society, we see that

Jewish women during the time of Jesus not only had a separate and different role from men but also one which was subordinate and inferior as well. It will be particularly important to keep these images of life for Jewish women in mind as we study in the next chapter how Jesus treated women.

STUDY QUESTIONS FOR CHAPTER 3

1. It is difficult for us in our highly educated Western society to understand how the rabbis so greatly influenced their culture. To identify more clearly with first-century Judaism, imagine that things are today as they were then. Imagine that your minister or priest is the only person in the neighborhood possessing written materials and the Scriptures. Imagine that he or she is the only one in the community who educates your children. With no public media available to you other than your clergyperson's readings and interpretations, how influential would he or she be in your life?

2. Some of the negative statements by rabbis after the time of Jesus regarding the birth of daughters are rather shocking. Have you ever seen cases today where the birth of a boy was considered more pleasing than the birth of a girl? Why do you suppose that was the case?

3. It is clear that under the ancient Jewish patriarchy the men were the leaders in all matters of life, while women functioned in supportive roles. Does our society still operate with similar assumptions today?

4. In the 1960s the United States Supreme Court made several landmark decisions about civil rights issues. The highest court ruled that the separation of black and white people in education does not foster equality. If separate is not equal in that case, what could you conclude about the relegation of women to the home in ancient Judaism?

Women and Jesus in the Gospels

Christendom understands that the most profound revelation of God's will for human relationships is discovered in the person of Jesus. As we look at Jesus' life from the perspective of the evangelists, we see a Jesus who demonstrated that women are to be treated equally with men.[1]

Mark

In Mark's witness to Jesus he shows Jesus to be one who was concerned for the welfare of women. Jesus praised the widow who gave her last mite (Mark 12:41-44; cf. Luke 21:1-4), and he denounced the scribes for taking financial advantage of widows in that city (Mark 12:40; cf. Matthew 23:1-36, Luke 20:45-47).

As we have seen, women were treated with a different standard than men in almost all Jewish laws. This was particularly true of laws concerning marriage and divorce.[2]

In Jesus' time, there were at least two rabbinical schools concerning divorce. One school, the Shammai school, held that the only grounds for divorce was sex offenses by the wife. The more liberal school of Hillel interpreted the grounds for divorce to be just about anything a husband did not like in his wife. Because of the contemporary controversy, the Pharisees asked Jesus if it was legal for a man to divorce his wife (Mark 10:2).[3] Instead of taking issue with the Shammai or Hillel schools, Jesus, according to Mark, explained the original purpose of marriage from Genesis: '' 'For this reason a man shall leave his father and mother and be joined to his wife, and the two shall become one flesh.' So they are no longer two but one flesh. What therefore God has joined together, let not man put asunder'' (Mark 10:7-9; cf. Matthew 19:5, 6).

In Mark's account (as well as in Matthew's) Jesus deals with the root of the problem of divorce rather than only with Jewish religious laws. He demonstrated that the obligations of a marriage relationship were extremely high. The idea of a man leaving his family and making the relationship with his wife more important than the relationship with his parents was probably difficult to consider for those in that male-oriented society. Jesus also was pointing out how men were treating women as things, divorcing them for any reason at all.

A particularly interesting incident was the healing of the woman with the hemorrhage.[4]

> And there was a woman who had had a flow of blood for twelve years, and who had suffered much under many physicians, and had spent all that she had, and was no better but rather grew worse. She had heard the reports about Jesus, and came up behind him in the crowd and touched his garment. For she said, "If I touch even his garments, I shall be made well." And immediately the hemorrhage ceased; and she felt in her body that she was healed of her disease. And Jesus, perceiving in himself that power had gone forth from him, immediately turned about in the crowd, and said, "Who touched my garments?" And his disciples said to him, "You see the crowd pressing around you, and yet you say, 'Who touched me?'" And he looked around to see who had done it. But the woman, knowing what had been done to her, came in fear and trembling and fell down before him, and told him the whole truth. And he said to her, "Daughter, your faith has made you well; go in peace, and be healed of your disease" (Mark 5:25-34; cf. Matthew 9:20-23; Luke 8:43-48).

Jesus must have been known as one so accepting that the troubled woman could approach him in faith. However timid she was, by reaching out to touch Jesus, she made a radical break with Jewish teaching. For a ritually "unclean" woman to approach and touch a man in public was a violation of all Jewish customs. How remarkable it was that Jesus then turned and called her "daughter," an intimate address! Likewise, Jesus restored the daughter of Jairus (Mark 5:22-24, 35-43; cf. Matthew 9:18-19, 23-26; Luke 8: 40-42, 49-56) and also healed Peter's mother-in-law (Mark 1:29-31; cf. Matthew 8:14-15; Luke 4: 38-39).

Another striking incident presented by two of the evangelists is Jesus' conversation with a non-Jewish woman.[5]

> And from there he arose and went away to the region of Tyre and Sidon. And he entered a house, and would not have any one know it; yet he could not be hid. But immediately a woman, whose little daughter was possessed by an unclean spirit, heard of him, and came and fell down at his feet. Now the woman was a Greek, a Syrophoenician by birth. And she begged him to cast the demon out of her daughter. And he said to her, "Let the children first be fed, for it is not right to take the children's bread and throw it to the dogs." But she answered him, "Yes, Lord; yet even the dogs under the table eat the children's crumbs." And he said to her, "For this saying you may go your way; the demon has left your daughter." And she went home, and found the child lying in bed, and the demon gone (Mark 7:24-30; cf. Matthew 15:21-28 and the discussion later in this chapter.)

Some commentators have tried to make Jesus' words less sharp than they were. But the fact remains that Jesus *appeared* to reject her outright as a non-Jew. Despite Jesus' apparent disinterest, she was even more adamant in her pleas for help. She dared to take Jesus at his word, and as a creature of God she claimed her right to God's mercy. The significance of the story for Mark seems to be that she was a Gentile and she believed her Creator could still show mercy toward her.

It was this woman's intellectual and emotional fortitude and faith in the face of rejection that enabled her to obtain her goal. Matthew's account, as we will see, emphasizes further her determination. Only one other time in the Gospel narratives is it portrayed that Jesus described someone's faith as being great.[6]

Matthew

Matthew includes most of Mark's material about Jesus' concern for women. In the teaching material of Jesus, Matthew alone includes Jesus' example about the ten virgins (Matthew 25: 1-13). It is significant that Jesus used women as examples in a culture that excluded women from educational activities. This is even more pronounced in Luke's material, as we will discuss later.

In Matthew's account of Jesus' teaching on divorce, he alone adds the possibility of divorce and remarriage for one whose first wife was unfaithful (Matthew 19:9). Jesus' words about the responsibilities in marriage so impressed the disciples, according to Matthew, that they seriously asked themselves whether it might be better to remain un-married (Matthew 19:10).

According to the evangelists' portrayal of Jesus' thought, under God's reign women were considered to be equal participants with men. In reference to future events, Jesus talked of how people would be suddenly taken by surprise (Matthew 24:37f.; Luke 17:35f.). Women, as well as men, would be included in life beyond death. An ongoing relationship with the eternal God, according to Jesus, is as much a reality for women as for men.[7]

In Matthew's account of Jesus meeting the Canaanite woman, the major point is the faith of a non-Jew, and a female non-Jew at that. He indicates that the woman knew that Jesus was the Messiah by her reference to "Son of David" (Matthew 15:22). He also gives additional detail to the story in his description of the woman braving the rejection of the disciples (v.23) as well as being confronted with Jesus' silence in response to her initial plea (v.23) and his statement of preference for the Jews (v.24).

As do the other evangelists, Matthew is careful to name some of the women who followed Jesus from Galilee (Matthew 27:55-56). Among them were Mary Magdalene, Mary the mother of James and Joseph, and the unnamed mother of the sons of Zebedee. Matthew also includes women in his genealogy of Jesus.

Luke

The real proof of what someone believes can be seen in that person's actions. In all of the Gospel narratives about Jesus' activity, it is apparent that he considered women to be equal with men. This is particularly evident in his healing ministry. Luke seems to have gone to greater lengths than the other Gospel writers to show some of Jesus' responses to women in particular. To mention a few of these responses, Luke alone describes Jesus' ministry to the widow of Nain (Luke 7:11-17). He had compassion for her (v.13) and then acted on the reason for her sorrow by raising her son to life. Jesus even risked "breaking" the sabbath in healing a lame woman (Luke 13:10-17).

Throughout the teachings of Jesus, women as well as men were used as illustrations. Luke portrayed Jesus' using everyday people in his object lessons, people with whom all in his audience, including women, could easily identify. Some of the parabolic characters included in Luke's teaching narratives were ordinary women: the woman who had lost the coin (Luke 15:8-10), the woman and the leaven (Luke

13:21), and the widow and the unjust judge (Luke 18:1-8). Jesus also used real characters as examples in his teachings. For instance, he praised the widow from Zarephath (Luke 4:25-26).

In the Lucan perspective perhaps the most outstanding incident showing Jesus' view of the role of women in religion occurred in the home of Mary and Martha.

> Now as they went on their way, he entered a village; and a woman named Martha received him into her house. And she had a sister called Mary, who sat at the Lord's feet and listened to his teaching. But Martha was distracted with much serving; and she went to him and said, "Lord, do you not care that my sister has left me to serve alone? Tell her then to help me." But the Lord answered her, "Martha, Martha, you are anxious and troubled about many things; one thing is needful. Mary has chosen the good portion, which shall not be taken away from her" (Luke 10:38-42).

In this passage Luke portrays Jesus as one who freely teaches a woman. In a culture that generally forbade women to sit and listen to a rabbi, here Jesus is shown to be giving theological education to a woman. It is highly significant that Luke portrays the scene of a woman receiving teaching with such detail. When Martha complained that her sister was not helping with the household responsibilities, Jesus defined the priorities. Even though both women may have been raised to view household duties as their most important tasks in life (besides raising a family), Jesus said that there was something more important. He mildly reminded Martha that homemaking should not be her highest priority. Rather, Jesus demonstrated that a person's spiritual and intellectual growth were of utmost importance. In this incident, Jesus is presented as teaching that it was more important for the women to learn about their faith than to be wrapped up only in ordinary day-to-day concerns.

It is probable that in Jesus' time the value of women was appreciated only in the areas of homemaking and propagation of the race. But when a woman remarked that Jesus' mother was blessed in her motherhood, Jesus quickly corrected the statement (Luke 11:27-28). His mother, or any other person for that matter, found true blessing in hearing the word of God and keeping it. Here Jesus was defining women's blessings as full participation in doing God's will.

In the narrative where Jesus dined with Simon the Pharisee (Luke 7:36f.),[8] Luke shows Simon as regarding the woman only as a worthless individual. But Jesus rebuked the Pharisee for not seeing that she was a person capable of being reconciled with God.

Jesus' ministry was a traveling ministry. Luke emphasized that along with the twelve disciples, there were also women who accompanied him (Luke 8:1-3). Apparently the women who traveled with Jesus shared in the ministry of Jesus because they provided for some expenses "out of their means" (Luke 8:3).

In Luke's Gospel Jesus did send out seventy men (Luke 10), and there were twelve male disciples; but it could hardly have been another way. Women would not have been able to travel because of the danger and lack of acceptance in the social structure of their male-dominated society. It cannot be denied, however, that, according to Luke, Jesus had women disciples traveling with him.

Throughout his ministry, Jesus openly demonstrated an appreciation for women's spiritual and intellectual capabilities as well as for their abilities to serve effectively. It may be significant that one of Jesus' last statements on his way to his execution, according to Luke, was made to women (Luke 23:27-30).

All of the evangelists describe the presence of women in their resurrection narratives. Luke, especially, seems to take an interest in the role of women in his account.

> And they found the stone rolled away from the tomb, but when they went in they did not find the body. While they were perplexed about this, behold, two men stood by them in dazzling apparel; and as they were frightened and bowed their faces to the ground, the men said to them, "Why do you seek the living among the dead? Remember how he told you, while he was still in Galilee, that the Son of man must be delivered into the hands of sinful men, and be crucified, and on the third day rise." And they remembered his words, and returning from the tomb they told all this to the eleven and to all the rest. Now it was Mary Magdalene and Joanna and Mary the mother of James and the other women with them who told this to the apostles; but these words seemed to them an idle tale, and they did not believe them (Luke 24:2-11).

The resurrection passage in the third Gospel contains significant material regarding the role of women in the life of Jesus and the church. In Luke's handling of the resurrection tradition, one sees a concern for the feminine segment of society. Luke arranges the sequence of the Sunday morning events to combine the discovery of the open tomb with the angelic announcement. While he does not include, or was not aware of, the account of Jesus' appearance to Mary Magdalene (according to John), he provides an account of similar happenings in the Emmaus pericope following (Luke 24:13-35).

As Luke tells it, apparently what the women were to remember (vv. 6 and 8) were Jesus' words predicting the passion and the resurrection (Luke 9:22; 18:32-33). After the resurrection the disciples themselves remember (Luke 24:6, 8), but here it is the women who first remember what Jesus had told them.[9]

John

John's Gospel shows Jesus' positive attitude toward women in his encounter with the Samaritan woman at the well. This happens to be the longest private conversation of Jesus with an individual as presented in any of the Gospels.

> He came to a city of Samaria, called Sychar, near the field that Jacob gave to his son Joseph. Jacob's well was there, and so Jesus, wearied . . . with his journey, sat down beside the well. It was about the sixth hour.
>
> There came a woman of Samaria to draw water. Jesus said to her, "Give me a drink." For his disciples had gone away into the city to buy food. The Samaritan woman said to him, "How is it that you, a Jew, ask a drink of me, a woman of Samaria?" For Jews have no dealings with Samaritans. . . .
>
> The woman said to him, "Sir, I perceive that you are a prophet. Our fathers worshiped on this mountain; and you say that in Jerusalem is the place where men ought to worship." Jesus said to her, "Woman, believe me, the hour is coming when neither on this mountain nor in Jerusalem will you worship the Father. . . . But the hour is coming, and now is, when the true worshipers will worship the Father in spirit and truth, for such the Father seeks to worship him. God is spirit, and those who worship him must worship in spirit and truth." The woman said to him, "I know that Messiah is coming (he who is called Christ); when he comes, he will show us all things." Jesus said to her, "I who speak to you am he."
>
> Just then his disciples came. They marveled that he was talking with a woman. . . .
>
> Many Samaritans from that city believed in him because of the woman's testimony, "He told me all that I ever did." So when the Samaritans came to him, they asked him to stay with them; and he stayed there two days. And many more believed because of his word (John 4:5-9, 19-21, 23-27a, 39-41).

In Jesus' conversation with this Samaritan woman he did three noticeable things: he openly talked to a woman in public; he, a Jew, spoke warmly with a Samaritan; and he engaged in teaching a woman. The contrast between his actions and what was perhaps considered acceptable by his culture is seen in the reaction of his disciples (John 4:27). They were actually surprised that he was even talking to the woman. But it was on the basis of this woman's testimony that many from Sychar believed the gospel.

John says that it was to Martha, the sister of Lazarus, that Jesus taught a point crucial to his entire ministry, the power of God to conquer even death. "I am the resurrection and the life; he who believes in me, though he die, yet shall he live, and whoever lives and believes in me shall never die. Do you [Martha] believe this?" (John 11:25-26).

John provides unique detail of Jesus' mother, Mary, at the crucifixion (John 19:26-27). The evangelist also adds some unique details involving Mary Magdalene to his resurrection account.

> But Mary stood weeping outside the tomb, and as she wept she stooped to look into the tomb; and she saw two angels in white, sitting where the body of Jesus had lain, one at the head and one at the feet. They said to her, "Woman, why are you weeping?" She said to them, "Because they have taken away my Lord, and I do not know where they have laid him." Saying this, she turned round and saw Jesus standing, but she did not know that it was Jesus. Jesus said to her, "Woman, why are you weeping? Whom do you seek?" Supposing him to be the gardener, she said to him, "Sir, if you have carried him away, tell me where you have laid him, and I will take him away." Jesus said to her, "Mary." She turned and said to him in Hebrew, "Rabboni!" (which means Teacher). . . .
> Mary Magdalene went and said to the disciples, "I have seen the Lord"; and she told them that he had said these things to her (John 20:11-16, 18; cf. Matthew 28:1-10).

It can be concluded, then, that, according to the Gospel narratives, women were the first to know that in Jesus' resurrection God had conquered death. Women were also the first witnesses to carry the good news of Jesus' resurrection.

Jesus openly included women in his religious instruction. He treated women as equally important participants in the plan of God. Jesus was the great liberator of all people, women included. He began his ministry proclaiming that he had been anointed "to set at liberty those who are oppressed" (Luke 4:18). Jesus' life and ministry literally demonstrated Galatians 3:28: "There is neither Jew nor Greek, there is neither slave nor free, there is neither male nor female; for you are all one in Christ Jesus."

Because Jesus dared to see women as human beings having equal rights with men, he can rightly be called a feminist.[10] Jesus' acceptance of women as free and responsible persons in his ministry is an important model to remember. Although Jesus is shown making no statements as to the teaching or authoritative status of women in the church, the evangelists' multiple witnesses to his life portray him as treating women and men as equals. This egalitarian behavior should be remembered in any discussion of women in church and society.

STUDY QUESTIONS FOR CHAPTER 4

1. For what reasons would the disciples not believe the reports of the women returning from the empty tomb?

2. Probably hundreds of women had heard Jesus' sermons. What do you think their response was after hearing someone use illustrations with which they, as women, could identify? Does this have any applications for preaching and teaching Scripture today in the church?

3. Jesus had a lot of close social contact with women. What does Jesus' inclusion of women in his activities have to say about the "men's Bible study" or the "women's groups" in churches today? Is that kind of segregation always necessary or healthy? In what circumstances is it helpful to restrict groups to one sex?

4. In light of the strong direction taken by Jesus, many denominations in our time have changed their policies concerning women in pastoral roles. Does your church view women as equal to men? Do women generally feel free to use their gifts for God? If not, in what ways could your church move in this direction?

Women in Paul's Letters

Jesus' practice of viewing men and women as equals continued on in the life of the early church. Unlike his Jewish contemporaries, Paul approved of women holding responsible positions in the church. He mentioned that Euodia and Syntyche had labored side by side with him in the gospel (Philippians 4:2-3). We also know that Christians benefited from the leadership of various women because of the ten women mentioned in Romans 16. Seven of the women are commended; four are called "hard workers in the gospel ministry" (Romans 16:6, 12); Junias is called noteworthy among the apostles,[1] and Phoebe is referred to as a deaconess (vv. 1-2).

It is clear from 1 Corinthians 11:5 that women were leading in prayer and prophesying in church services (although the difficulties in the text will be discussed). The purpose of prophecy was, in all probability, what we know to be the purpose of preaching today: "upbuilding and encouragement and consolation" (1 Corinthians 14:3).

To participate fully in worship was a new experience for first-century Jewish-Christian women. Formerly they had to remain behind screens in the synagogue service where they were spectators rather than active participants. Now they had the opportunity to pray aloud and speak directly to other worshipers in the congregation. However, some problems arose in the Corinthian church.[2] In 1 Corinthians 11, Paul addresses a problem pertaining to the wearing of veils.

> But I want you to understand that the head of every man is Christ, the head of a woman is her husband, and the head of Christ is God. Any man who prays or prophesies with his head covered dishonors his head, but any woman who prays or prophesies with her head unveiled dishonors her head—it is the same as if her head were shaven. For if a woman will not veil herself, then she should cut off her hair; but if it is disgraceful for a woman to be shorn or shaven, let her wear a veil. For a man ought not to cover his head, since he is the image and glory of God; but woman is the glory of man. (For man was not made from woman, but woman from man.) Neither was man created for woman, but woman for man. That is why a woman ought to have a veil on her head, because of the angels. (Nevertheless, in the Lord woman is not independent of man nor man of woman; for as woman was made from man, so man is now born of woman. And all things are from God.) Judge for yourselves: is it proper for a woman to pray to God with her head uncovered? Does not nature itself teach you that for a man to wear long hair is degrading to him, but if a woman has long hair, it is her pride? For her hair is given to her for a covering. If anyone is disposed to be contentious, we recognize no other practice, nor do the churches of God (1 Corinthians 11:3-16).[3]

Often this difficult and elusive passage has been interpreted to indicate a man's authority over his wife based on the order of creation (1 Corinthians 11:7-9). Traditionally some commentators have argued that since man was made first and is in God's image and since woman is thought to be made in man's image but not God's (although there is no text to support this reasoning), woman is then thought to be subordinate to man.[4] Further, since man was created in God's image and woman in man's (supposedly), it is often next interpreted that woman was not in God's image and is, therefore, not quite up to the level of man.[5] The wearing of a veil then reminds women that they are to remain under the authority of their husbands. This traditional interpretation, however, would seem to run counter to what we already know of Paul's view of women.

The two issues that are difficult for us to understand in this text are the husband's headship and the function of veils. Paul's use of the word for "head" or "source" (kephalē) in the context of the husband-wife relationship was not used to mean a hierarchy in the relationship.

There are only two places kephalē is used in connection with a husband and wife relationship: in this passage and probably by another author in Ephesians 5:23-24. Elsewhere kephalē is used to refer to the head of a human being, and five times Christ is called the head of the corner as in Matthew 21:42. The body is also spoken of as growing from the head (Ephesians 4:16; Colossians 2:19) as well as saving the body (Ephesians 5:23).[6] It is emphasized in Colossians 2:9-10 that Christ is the head or the *source* of the lifeblood of the church. This understanding of the word seems to be an acceptable meaning, especially as we look at the whole of this passage.[7] Here it describes the intimacy in marriage to be like Christ's relationship to God the Creator (1 Corinthians 11:3).

The particular problem in this Corinthian house church was that women were removing their customary veils during the worship. Paul was concerned that this new freedom for women was bordering on bad taste. In the first-century culture, certain hairstyles and the wearing of veils signified that a woman was married, much like the wearing of a wedding ring does today. According to the Jewish Talmud, if women abandoned their veils, they flaunted their marriage vows. This constituted grounds for divorce.[8]

In 1 Corinthians 11:2 Paul asks them to "maintain the [Jewish] traditions even as I have delivered them to you." Then in verses 4 through 6 he summarizes some of the Jewish worship customs, namely, that men are to pray and speak publicly without their heads, covered and women are to wear the customary veils. The argument here is that it is just as disgraceful for a woman to go unveiled as it would be for her to be shaved (v.5).[9] Therefore, the woman should be sure to wear a veil. If not, he suggests, why not cut her hair off (v.6), which, presumably, no woman would consider doing in that culture. Further, Paul may have been making sure that Christian worship services would not be confused by outsiders with the pagan services that involved sexually immoral priestesses of the Aphrodite cult who did not wear veils. This congregation's testimony in the pagan city of Corinth perhaps concerned Paul so much that he resorted to additional arguments in order to change their apparent disregard for veils in church.[10]

In verses 7-9, Paul employs a theological argument for women to wear veils. Man is in the image of God, and woman is the glory of man; but this does not imply that woman is more distant from God's image than man. If so, Paul would have completed the parallelism that woman is in the *image* of man instead of the *glory* of man.[11] Woman, as well as man, was created in the image of God (Genesis 1:27). Because woman was originally made as a helper-companion for man, who alone could not replenish the earth (Genesis 1:28), she is different. Paul is not saying that the man is the lord and master of the woman;

he is saying that man was the origin of her being in creation, remembering that woman was said, in the creation imagery, to be made from the man's rib.[12] Therefore, Paul's reasoning is that women are to show their distinction from men in creation by use of a veil. The veil, then, is a witness to the authority of the Creator who made man and woman different. It signifies her difference in the flow of creation and perhaps one thing further: her newfound authority. Bruce notes that in the synagogue service of worship a quorum of ten (formerly ten males) was necessary for worship to begin.[13] Since Christian women are considered equal with men in Christ (Galatians 3:28) and since they may now pray and prophesy at meetings, a woman's veil could also signify the new authority of women to stand beside men under God.

In short, Paul may be using the veil custom (which formerly meant subjection to men in those times) to mean several things: (1) that Christian women in worship are not like the immoral women of that time who do not wear veils; (2) that there is a closeness in creation between man and woman; yet they are distinct as sexes, and (3) in observing the use of veils, women proclaim their prominent place in creation as the glory of men, who are their source in creation.[14] In this way, the ordinary social significance of veils would be transcended. "As man in public worship manifests his authority by leaving his head unveiled, so woman manifests hers by wearing a veil."[15]

Paul gives a further reason for veils by appealing to the presence of angels (1 Corinthians 11:10). The reference to angels has been interpreted in relation to Genesis 6:1-4 where "sons of God" (angels) were said to assault women. This notion that veils are to protect worshiping women from evil angels seems somewhat far-fetched.[16]

An alternative and perhaps more plausible view is that Paul sees angels as guardians of the created order.[17] In light of the previous discussion of the distinctiveness of men and women in the order of creation (1 Corinthians 11:7), Paul is perhaps reminding this congregation that the form of this world has not yet passed away (1 Corinthians 7:26-31) and that the world's categories of orderliness have not become obsolete.[18]

The authority (*exousia*) symbolized by the woman's head covering is the new authority women themselves have through Christ, the authority of God on their lives. Paul thinks that because woman is man's glory, her head must be covered to hide the glory of man in the presence of God and God's angels. "If she were to pray or prophesy with uncovered head, she would not be glorifying God, but reflecting the glory of man, and in God's presence this must inevitably turn to shame." [19]

Therefore, Paul's teaching suggests that women should see that their physical presence does not distract the attention of other worshipers from their focus on God. This certainly does not indicate that women today should wear veils or hats, as some have insisted, or any other outmoded style of dress. It does suggest, however, that women should not dress specifically and solely to attract attention to themselves. The same principle should apply directly to men as well.

Perhaps to insure that his readers do not begin to think that head coverings indicate women's subjection to men, Paul reinforces the concept of mutuality in 1 Corinthians 11:11-12. Just as woman found her origin in man (v.8), man is to remember that he in turn comes through the woman. Each then owes existence to and cannot exist without the other.[20] Likewise, all men and women owe their existence to God.

In verses 13-15, Paul returns to the "it's natural" argument in support of women wearing veils. He rhetorically asks them to judge for themselves what is proper. He implies his answer to be correct, suggesting that long hair on women is a natural head covering for the reasons mentioned in verses 7-8. He winds up his exhortations to this church by saying that what he has said is normative in the other local congregations (v.16).

Paul was greatly concerned with the tendency of this congregation to be insensitive to social customs. Outsiders might be misled to think that Christian worship involved pagan practices. Further, Paul strongly believed that veils symbolized a natural dignity of woman in relation to man in creation.

Paul's theological reasoning for veils for the sake of creation (vv. 7-9) and for the angels (v.10) was probably easily understood by that congregation since he had spoken to them on many occasions. Biblical scholars today, however, continue to struggle to understand more fully this brief and puzzling passage. But despite the difficulties of this passage, Paul at least appears to be arguing for their adherence to the veil custom because of a positive and high view of women rather than the opposite. Paul didn't want the Corinthian Christians to do something that was disgraceful (v.6) or unnatural (v.14) because women, as distinct beings from men, share a glory (v.7) in creation that should be reflected even in the customs of the worshiping community.

Paul addressed yet another problem pertaining to women in the church.

> For God is not a God of confusion but of peace.
> As in all the churches of the saints, the women should keep silence in the churches. For they are not permitted to speak, but should be subordinate, even as the law says. If there is anything they desire to know, let them ask their husbands at home. For it is shameful for a woman to speak in church. What! Did the word of God originate with you, or are you the only ones it has reached? . . . all things should be done decently and in order (1 Corinthians 14:33-35, 40).

Because verse 37 links up better with verse 32 and the content of verses 33-36 seems to be an interruption of Paul's discussion on prophecy in the chapter, many scholars believe this passage is an addition of later scribes.[21]

It is clear, however, that women were praying and prophesying in the services (1 Corinthians 11:5).[22] The specific problem being discussed is that certain women in that church were interrupting the services by asking questions and carrying on discussions. Because many of the Jewish traditions continued to be observed in the early churches, Christians worshiped in much the same way as they had in the synagogues.[23] In first-century churches, men sat on one side of the church and women on the other. Some wives, then, may have called across the aisle to their husbands, indicating their approval of a particular point in the sermon. Some women, so anxious to express themselves in the service, got carried away and interrupted the worship with their conversations. This may be why those women were instructed to wait until they got home for discussion (1 Corinthians 14:35).

To emphasize further the importance of orderliness in worship, the text mentions that Jewish tradition taught women to subordinate their personal interests to the higher priority of worship and study of the Torah "even as the law says" (1 Corinthians 14:34).

However, the passage clearly was requesting the women to be subordinate in the traditional sense, much in the same way church leaders later suggested in the pastoral epistles. However, if this scribal addition was understood to be prohibiting all Christian women from participating in leading in worship, it would be totally inconsistent with all Paul had said about the women who led in various churches and contrary to his teachings about the equality of women with men. "There is neither Jew nor Greek, there is neither slave nor free, there is neither male nor female; for you are all one in Christ Jesus" (Galatians 3:28).

Therefore, we can begin to see some tension between Paul's readiness to accept women in church leadership and the more traditional role expectation of the second- or third-generation church leaders, as we will discuss later.

STUDY QUESTIONS FOR CHAPTER 5

1. In Paul's writings there are cases in which a few individuals caused interruptions in the worship services of various congregations. Can you think of experiences you have had in your church where some have dominated Bible studies and not permitted others to participate? What would you say is the proper way to handle such situations?

2. Think about the possibility of your church hiring a woman minister if it does not presently have one. What would be the advantages of having a woman assume responsibility for preaching, marriage counseling, teaching, and in other areas? How would the congregation react? Are such reactions valid?

3. What do you think the Christian church will eventually do in terms of giving women full leadership responsibilities in ministry? What are you personally doing to move the church in this direction?

4. In what ways do you think that secular society is ahead of the church in giving women and men equal status?

Women in Ephesians 5

Christians made a startling break with their Jewish heritage in their teachings about marriage. The groundwork for a totally new understanding of how people are to relate to one another in marriage is seen in Ephesians 5:

> Be subject to one another out of reverence for Christ. Wives, be subject to your husbands, as to the Lord. For the husband is the head of the wife as Christ is the head of the church, his body, and is himself its Savior. As the church is subject to Christ, so let wives also be subject in everything to their husbands. Husbands, love your wives, as Christ loved the church and gave himself up for her, that he might sanctify her, having cleansed her by the washing of water with the word, that he might present the church to himself in splendor, without spot or wrinkle or any such thing, that she might be holy and without blemish. Even so husbands should love their wives as their own bodies. He who loves his wife loves himself. For no man ever hates his own flesh, but nourishes and cherishes it, as Christ does the church, because we are members of his body. "For this reason a man shall leave his father and mother and be joined to his wife and the two shall become one flesh." This mystery is a profound one, and I am saying that it refers to Christ and the church; however, let each one of you love his wife as himself, and let the wife see that she respects her husband (Ephesians 5:21-33).[1]

Traditionally these verses have been interpreted as assigning wives

71

total submission to their husbands and husbands the responsibility to love (but not submit to) their wives.[2] Commentators have gone on to say that since the husband is the "head," it means that he is the head of the house (in the authoritarian sense) and that a wife is to submit to her husband's final say on all matters. To avoid the possibility of promoting a dictatorship, this argument is careful to note that husbands should be loving in their rule over the marriage.

This interpretation of the word "head" *(kephalē)* and this understanding of the point of the passage have had some impractical consequences in Christian marriages. As a minister I have been involved in much marriage counseling before and after weddings and divorces. Often a couple's understanding of the husband as "head" of the house is this: While both are to be involved in every important decision, the man is to have the final say on the very important issues. Couples feel that to designate a "final say" is some kind of necessary safeguard against possible stalemates in critical matters.

Following this line of reasoning, I next ask couples how they would determine what is an important enough issue that the husband can veto even his wife's strongest thoughts and feelings. And always, in every case, there is a confused and lasting silence in response to that question. "Head of the house" is a meaningless term for many in our society today. In no marriage relationship, where it is agreed that both are to be equal, can there ever be a practical line drawn so that one person always has the "last say" about any category or decision. While many couples try to live this way, it only leads to frustration on the part of the wife and an overburdening responsibility to be perfect on the part of the husband.

The overall point of Ephesians 5:21-33 is summarized in 5:21 and again in verse 33. In a Christian marriage, *both* husband and wife are to be subject to one another (see Colossians 3:18–4:1). Verses 22 through 24 of Ephesians 5 speak to wives, and a longer passage from verses 25 through 33 instructs husbands.

In the advice to Christian wives, this text does something that most people in the first century might have expected. It instructs women to obey their husbands.[3] The Jewish men and other Gentile male converts to the faith would be familiar with this teaching. First-century Jews and pagans probably had grown up with the teaching that women needed to be reminded how to live.

But as Markus Barth points out, this admonition is not that all women are to submit to all men. Rather, Christian wives are to submit only to their husbands, and only in a framework of mutual submission.[4] The very suggestion of both submitting to one another (v.21) infers that it is a voluntary act of two free agents, not a "subjugation which denies, breaks or obliterates the will of the subjected party."[5] In short, the submission is to be as one submits to Christ "as to the Lord" (v.22). One submits to his or her partner because it is fitting as a Christian, and one's submission is to parallel Christ's total giving of himself to the church (vv. 25-30).[6]

Although the authority concept may have been intended (as in Ephesians 1:22-23), this passage does not seem to be talking in terms of a hierarchy. Rather, the word for "head" seems to mean *source* rather than authority.[7] Therefore, the writer of Ephesians seems to be using the term *source* to say that the closeness in a marriage relationship is to parallel the closeness in a believer's relationship with Christ. The description of Christ's relationship to the body reflects the notion that the head gives the body its life and saves it from destruction.[8] So a closer translation of verses 22 and 23 might read: "Wives, be subject to your husbands just as you are to the Lord, for just as Christ is the *source* of the church's (existence), and is himself its savior, likewise, the husband is the source for the wife." These verses should never be read alone but always in the context of verse 21 which says *both* are to submit to one another.

Perhaps this picture of unity between man and woman is a reflection on Genesis 2:18-23, which poetically portrays Eve as being made from part of Adam's body.[9] There was a special bond Eve had with Adam as he was, in that sense, her source of life. However, it would be unwarranted to infer that the word "source" always implies a ranking.[10] Because an infant has his or her source of life through a mother, there is a unity or bond and yet certainly an equality of the two. The same is to be true in marriage. The author seems to be saying, then, that just as people in the church find their motivation in the faith in Christ, so, too, a wife should be motivated toward happiness in marriage by her husband. In short, the union that believers have in Christ should be reflected in marriage.

In further discussion Ephesians 5:25-33 suggests that a husband's relationship to his wife is to be like Christ's relationship to the church. That is, Christ gave his body to save the church (Ephesians 5:23). Christ was the savior and redeemer of the church. Therefore, a man should be willing to sacrifice anything for his wife, just as Jesus did for the church. Christ's headship in the church is one which does not dominate. Rather it nourishes (v.25) and enables the church to grow in unity (Ephesians 4:15-16). While it is clear that Christ's headship over the church can be viewed as a reign (Ephesians 1:19-23), Ephesians 5 emphasizes the *serving* nature of Jesus' relationship to the church in illustrating a husband's behavior toward his wife.

While the advice to wives may have been expected, the advice to husbands is quite unusual (Ephesians 5:25-33). Unlike much in Jewish writings for centuries, this passage teaches that marriage involves a mutual commitment of giving. In fact, elsewhere, when the New Testament discusses the behavior of wives, it gives similar instructions to the husbands (1 Corinthians 7:4; 11:1, 12; 1 Peter 3:7). A man is to love his spouse as he loves and cares for his own body (Ephesians 5:28). In the same way, women are urged to be "subject" to their husbands. "For the wife does not rule over her own body, but the husband does; likewise the husband does not rule over his own body, but the wife does" (1 Corinthians 7:4). This relationship between a Christian husband and wife is a mystery in the author's mind (Ephesians 5:32). This mutuality in the relationship is so unlike what appears to be normative in Judaism at the time that the author has resorted to a lengthy discussion using the metaphor of Christ's relationship to the church.

The point then is that *all* Christians are to be subject to one another, not just women to men. Both wives and husbands are urged to be subject to one another (v.21). Wives are urged to be subject to their husbands, while husbands are instructed to give themselves totally to their wives, even to the point of following Christ's example of self-sacrifice. This quality of love is the most profound illustration of what submission is.[11]

It is interesting that the following sentence continues to expand this model for other relationships. Children are to obey their parents (Ephesians 6:1-3), and, conversely, fathers are not to be overbearing (v.4). Slaves are to obey those over them (vv.5-8), and, on the other hand, masters are to "do the same," which means to act as servants of Christ doing God's will (v.9). They are to remember that just as they are overseers of their slaves, God oversees their actions. While some concept of authority remains for parents and overseers of workers, all are to remember that Christ's example of authority was not characterized by power over people but by service.

It has been noted that if all Christian slave owners had strictly followed this advice, slavery would have disappeared sooner than it did. Perhaps also if Christian husbands had followed the advice of Ephesians 5:25-33, the tendency for them to dominate in the marriage relationship would have diminished long ago.

Whenever the New Testament mentions submission, it is not a reference to superiority and inferiority. Humility is the point, not passivity or a blind, unreasoned adherence to whatever the other says. Ephesians 5 is saying that marriage is giving and receiving, not a rigid or fixed order of roles and duties. Marriage is to be an egalitarian relationship between a man and woman. It is not to be in the world's pattern of someone being dominant while the other is submissive. Men and women are not to lord it over one another (Mark 10:42-45) but are to be subject to one another out of reverence for Christ (Ephesians 5:21). With such attitudes there would never be disputes over authority or rights in a marriage.

It is certainly possible that the author of Ephesians went along with his first-century culture and assigned some sort of "final say" to husbands. In this society women had been denied education and access to society at large, and possibly in those times it was somewhat necessary for the more educated men to lead. There was certainly sympathy for the plight of women as their situation is referred to as "weaker" in 1 Peter 3:7: "Likewise you husbands, live considerately with your wives, bestowing honor on the woman as the weaker sex, since you are joint heirs of the grace of life, in order that your prayers may not be hindered." However, the overwhelming point of the teaching of Ephesians 5 is that in Christian marriage there is to be a mutual submission that parallels Christ's selfless giving to the church. This kind of love is to be the prevailing characteristic of a couple's marriage in carrying out tasks and making decisions.

Christianity brought with it new patterns for human relationships. In addition to Jesus' example in giving himself, the epistles also describe a new potential and way of living for women, men, children, parents, employers, and employees. While Christ and the church established these new possibilities, the world's patterns were not radically changed by the end of the first century. Slavery continued until the ninteenth century, and women continue to be dominated by men even today.

This brings us back to the question of the dynamics of a marriage of mutuality. Does one person have to have the last say?

Everyone is gifted in different areas, and at times one partner will have more developed thoughts and feelings on certain issues and tasks than the other. Marriage then is not a completed puzzle where all parts fit together to eliminate holes; rather, it is like the blending of diverse colors to form a beautiful picture. Obviously, it would be impractical and impossible for the wife and husband to sit down and together decide the outcome of every single issue. For convenience and economy of life-style, various tasks are relegated to one or the other in the marriage.The wife may take out the trash every week; the husband may mow the lawn, or vice versa. Whenever one spouse decides to take responsibility in an area, that decision is made according to the schedules, talents, interests, feelings, and physical abilities of both partners. There is no such thing as preordained "men's work" or "women's work." Because of the educational, social, and economic changes for women in our society, we need to realize that women are not living, nor will they ever again live, as they did in Hellenistic times or even as our grandparents or parents lived.

My wife is gifted in banking and finance. She once had a responsible position in a Massachusetts bank. Since her talent, interest, and desire are in that area, it would be foolish for me as a husband to insist on taking the major responsibility for money matters in our household, although we frequently discuss money matters together. One could say that my wife usually has the "last say" in our financial matters; it is not that way because she is the "head of the house." The same is true of decisions I make on matters in which I have greater interest or aptitude. I feel that our relationship is such that we both feel a close union, a mutual submission. While Ephesians 5 suggests that a man is a source for a woman in marriage, Christian men today are seeing their wives to be equally a source, or resource, for them as well.

STUDY QUESTIONS FOR CHAPTER 6

1. We don't have to look too far to see that many in our present-day society think that the husband is to be the head of the house in the authoritarian sense of that term. It is interesting in marriage counseling to ask couples what they mean when they designate the man as the "head." Can you think of any areas in the marriage relationship where a man should have the final say on a decision just because he is a man? If not, why not?

2. Some people feel that in human relationships one person always has to be dominant while the other always has to be submissive. In light of Ephesians 5, what sort of dynamic should be going on instead of the worldly dominance-submission pattern? Give some illustrations from your own experiences.

3. Why do you think the idea of the wife submitting to her husband has been emphasized more often than the idea of mutual submission of woman *and* man?

4. Ephesians 5 and 6 advise Christians to balance lopsided relationships in marriage, between parents and children, and in master-slave situations. Old forms of slavery have been largely eliminated today. Do you see any parallels to how changes in marriage and parent-child relationships would affect people's experiences of being a spouse or child or parent? How would these changes cause differences in the way conflicts are handled in these relationships?

5. "Senior" ministers often feel threatened by other ministers on the staff. The competition or fear of being outdone is often seen in the very fact that a second minister's title is usually "assistant" or "associate." We can see that not only do men think that they must be dominant in man-woman relationships but also in man-man relationships. What implications do the New Testament teachings on mutuality have for church employees, church leaders, and similar relationships in the business world?

6. Medical science shows us that today men are predominantly the ones who suffer from hypertension and coronary disease. Does the New Testament advice regarding mutual submission have any relevance for the aggressive, competitive tendency of today's life-style?

Women in Acts and the Pastoral Epistles

Chapter 7

Acts

As he did in the first half of his work, Luke demonstrated the prominent place of women in Acts. Women were specifically mentioned in connection with the Philippian and Thessalonian congregations (Acts 17:4), in Beroea (Acts 17:12), in Athens (Acts 17:34), and in the church at Corinth (Acts 18:2), suggesting that women were vital members of these congregations. It was Priscilla and her husband Aquila who instructed the gifted communicator Apollos (Acts 18:24-26; cf. Romans 16:3; 1 Corinthians 16:19; 2 Timothy 4:19). It is clear that women were respected in the early church and included in the congregations. "And more than ever believers were added to the Lord, multitudes both of men and women . . ." (Acts 5:14). When Greek-speaking Jewish widows in the Jerusalem church were in special need, deacons were appointed to meet that need (Acts 6:1-3).

While Paul was in Philippi on his second journey, a merchant woman named Lydia became a believer and led her family to the faith (Acts 16:14-15). Mary, the mother of John Mark, was one who opened her home for believers to meet (Acts 12:12). There can be no mistake that women as well as men even experienced persecution for the sake of Christ. See Saul's persecution in Acts 8:3 when he dragged off men

82   Speaking Out for Women

and women and committed them to prison.[1] In referring to all these prominent women in the early church, no distinction was made in roles acccording to sex.

Women had a significant role in the apocryphal literature.[2] Women disciples are frequently mentioned, and there are many dialogues between women and Jesus in these interesting and imaginative narratives. In fact, throughout apocryphal literature there is an intense interest in how Jesus and the apostles may have involved women in their ministry in incidents other than those recorded in the New Testament.[3]

But these changes in the early church caused growing pains. Christian women experienced a new freedom in the early congregations, but this freedom was not without its problems, as we have seen. This new liberating direction for women, however, was suggested earlier by the prophet Joel and, according to Luke, was applied by the apostles at Pentecost:

" 'And in the last days it shall be, God declares,
that I will pour out my Spirit upon all flesh,
and your sons and your daughters shall prophesy,
and your young men shall see visions,
and your old men shall dream dreams;
yea, and on my menservants and my maidservants in those days
I will pour out my Spirit; and they shall prophesy. . . .
And it shall be that whoever calls on the name of the Lord shall be
saved.' "

Acts 2:17-18, 21

The Pastoral Epistles[4]

Because women were destitute if they were widowed or divorced, a special order of widows was established at one period in the early church. In 1 Timothy 5:3-16, Timothy is advised to aid widows. Relatives were urged to provide for widowed women (5:8). Widows were enrolled in a special group with the understanding that they should be honored (5:3). They were encouraged to live up to high standards (5:10) and offer special prayers (5:5).[5] To live in accordance with God's will, it was taught, among other things, that one should visit widows (James 1:27).

Abuse sometimes comes with freedom. More and more women experienced new respectability in Christianity, but in the congregation addressed it appears that some women were abusing their newfound freedom.

Let a woman learn in silence with all submissiveness. I permit no woman to teach or to have authority over men; she is to keep silent. For Adam was formed first, then Eve; and Adam was not deceived, but the woman was deceived and became a transgressor. Yet woman will be saved through bearing children, if she continues in faith and love and holiness, with modesty (1 Timothy 2:11-15).

This passage is one of the most difficult statements to relate to the rest of the New Testament writings and obviously stands in tension with the writings of Paul. As in 1 Corinthians 11, it is unfortunate that the writer did not expand further on what was meant because the particular context of the problem which was being addressed remains uncertain.

The word translated "silence" (*ăsousea*) in verse 11 also means "quietness."[6] Nevertheless, women are clearly being told to be quiet in instructional times and to be submissive as in traditional Jewish custom (1 Timothy 2:11). Further, the word usually translated as "to have authority" (*authentein*) in verse 12 is not used anywhere else in the entire New Testament. Through studying other writings of the first century, scholars have found that the word means "to have authority over" or "to domineer over someone else." Before Paul's time, the word had to do with "having full power over" or "committing murder."[7] It is clear that the word is not the usual one for "authority" but is a rare and harsh verb. The larger creation argument, however, in verses 13-15 seems to restrict the behavior of women in general, and the writer clearly desires no woman to teach or have authority over the men of the congregation.[8]

It is possible that as the women in the congregation experienced this new permission to participate in the assembly, some violated basic courtesies necessary in learning and discussion. The violations seem to extend to some women's roles in teaching (v.12). We do not know the details of the congregation's particular situation, and we can only speculate; but some women may have been teaching in the church, and, in doing so, they may have been dominating and overbearing. It might be conjectured that these same women had become indoctrinated with heresy and wanted to teach it in the church.[9]

To emphasize this further, an illustration from another woman's experience is given (vv.11-15), as had been done by Paul in earlier writings: "But I am afraid that as the serpent deceived Eve by his cunning, your thoughts will be led astray from a sincere and pure devotion to Christ" (2 Corinthians 11:3). Likewise, the reader is asked to think about Adam and Eve. It is suggested that it was not Adam who was first deceived by untruth, but Eve. The writer, in fact, denies that Adam was deceived (1 Timothy 2:14) and appears to be harshly implying that women in general may be more prone to being deceived.[10] The point of the writer using this interpretation of the Genesis narrative probably was to remind the women that on another occasion someone was surprised to find out that she had been completely deceived by untruth. Perhaps the author wanted the women in this church to realize that they also had been deceived by their own sin, which exhibited domineering and disruptive behavior, in the opinion of the writer. It is likely, however, that the writer did not want women addressing the congregation even if they conducted themselves in an orderly and polite manner. "I permit *no* woman to teach or to have authority over men; she is to keep silent" (v.12, italics added).

This warning to these women continues (v.15): "Yet woman will be saved through bearing children. . . ." This is likely an admonition in keeping with Jewish tradition. It suggests that women should find their fulfillment through the traditional modes of being a mother and a subordinate wife in Judaism.[11] These women, then, the author is saying, should continue in the Christian "faith" (v.15) and exercise "love and holiness, with modesty."

The argument of this passage, then, seems to be a return to the traditional Jewish thought about the status of women in religion. While the harshness of the word used to describe the dominating behavior possibly of a few women can be observed, one cannot deny that the passage seeks to restrict women in the traditional Jewish subordinate role model. This tendency in the later church (possibly reflected also in the scribal addition of 1 Corinthians 14:33-35) stands in tension with the earlier Pauline writings.

Paul's writings seem to be based on understanding that women were to be participating with men in the church. Paul never attempted to restrict women's responsible participation in the first-century congregations. Rather, he praised women as leaders in the gospel ministry and spoke of the beneficial work they were doing.

These two diverging viewpoints in the New Testament demonstrate some of the dialogue going on between the different generations of the early church. As Christians attempted to hammer out the relevance of their faith in their own time, there were certainly tensions in the process. As was reflected in Acts, in the early church there was considerable disagreement as to whether Gentiles should receive the gospel.

We would conclude, then, that women were actively participating in some Christian congregations in contrast to earlier traditions. The extent of their participation, however, is unclear. Although there is considerable tension in the epistles regarding the proper conduct of women in the church, it seems clear that in some situations women did serve as leaders but probably only to a limited extent because of first-century customs.

First-century Christianity brought an opportunity at least in some places for women to participate increasingly in religious faith and worship. It is true that many of the male-dominated traditions, such as excluding women from leadership roles, continued to be observed during the first few centuries.[12] On the other hand, Christianity, unlike many earlier religions, offered women a chance to participate, paving the way for full equality for women and men in the future.

However, the assertion in Genesis 3:16, that men will tend to dominate women, has held true throughout the centuries, sadly enough even in the church. The church in later centuries has tended to ignore the fact that women had leadership roles in the early church. While the church has made a great leap forward in including women in most parts of congregational life, it has failed to assist women to continue on in the direction toward full equality begun in the first century.

Scripture demonstrates that both Jesus and Paul modeled a new equalizing direction for women. While the entire world was not turned upside down and all injustices corrected, the Spirit of God was at least moving people in a new direction, especially with regard to the status of women. It is our task as Christians, then, to perceive this direction in Scripture and to try to bring about similar changes in our society.

STUDY QUESTIONS FOR CHAPTER 7

1. Our interpretations of difficult biblical passages sometimes change. In commenting on the 1 Timothy 2 passage, John Calvin in 1546 said: "Unquestionably whenever even natural propriety has been maintained, women have in all ages been excluded from the public management of affairs. It is the dictate of common sense that female government is improper and unseemly." [13] If his interpretation had been maintained until now, what would have to change in the church?

2. The New Testament is not a document with a single view on any given matter. What would have happened if the majority of the church had continued to refuse to take the gospel to the Gentiles? (See Acts 15.)

Beginning

Chapter 8

We are living in exciting times, and Christians have much to be confident about. God is at work, and despite the widespread injustices in relationships between women and men, there is hope. But God's work in correcting injustice has not always been as fast as we would like. It took considerable argument and debate in the first Christian church in Jerusalem before they validated Paul's taking the gospel to the Gentiles (Acts 15). Luke, and Paul in Galatians, supported that broadening emphasis. It was not until as late as the nineteenth century that the oppressiveness of slavery was effectively confronted by the church. And now, in our lifetime, the church is slowly but definitely seeing that there is no male and female dichotomy in Christ (Galatians 3:28).

Still, I have talked with several women who have completed their Master of Divinity degrees and have contributed to many people's lives through their church-related field work. But when these women were interviewed for church jobs, they almost universally were asked degrading questions. Church pulpit committees have a tendency to interview women as if they are emotionally unbalanced, unlearned individuals who have only a glimmer of theological understanding. Many pulpit committees disregard women's dossiers altogether.

A number of churches exclude women from even serving on church boards. The sad fact is that there are millions of women whose gifts are being wasted. Perhaps this denial of women's talent and leadership has been a large factor in the lack of growth in some congregations.

Jesus Christ has shown us that there is to be a new order of life that liberates the oppressed (Luke 4:18). It is the presence of God's reign that allows no racial, social, or sexual discrimination. Although Jesus made no explicit statements about women's leadership roles, his actions shockingly challenged the norms of his time. He profoundly demonstrated that women were to be treated with equality. The same is to be true of our lives as well.

Parts of the early church moved in a *direction* that gave women freedom to lead and participate. The church today is called to continue in this direction. Just as we saw women being active in parts of the early church, there need be no hesitation today concerning women church school teachers, deacons, elders, or ministers. Fortunately, this has been the standard practice of many main-line denominations for more than half of this century.

Christians who submit to biblical authority are called, like Jesus, to step ahead of the culture and seek to liberate all people, rich and poor, black and white, female and male. The time is overdue for Christian leaders to stop wrenching isolated scriptural passages out of their literary and historical contexts. It is certainly time for the church to start treating the female 51 percent with a dignity equal to that which Jesus so outstandingly demonstrated.

The clergy and others who speak to or for the church need to attempt to communicate fully to everyone in their audiences. Perhaps male speakers need to read women's magazines from time to time to become aware of women's concerns. All communicators need to strive to use illustrations with which women, as well as men, can easily identify.

Worship leaders also can work on the language used in sermons, in hymns, and in liturgy. It is clear that the writers of the Bible most often thought of God in terms of "he" and God's followers as "men" even when both men and women were intended. While this language was used in the generic sense by biblical writers, it is important in our application to contemporary life to avoid limiting God to masculine imagery and male pronouns. We now need to change our pronouns and make our language more explicitly inclusive. We are not to be embarrassed to change the Scripture wording to "people" instead of "men" where the Greek and Hebrew allow for it. We are not to shy away from changing hymn lyrics that seem to exclude women. For instance, "Rise Up, O *Men* of God" can be "Rise Up, O *Saints* of God" (italics added). Scripture clearly portrays God as Spirit who manifests androgynous (both feminine and masculine) attributes.

Christian women are realizing that merely being cynical about sexism in their experiences actually perpetuates the injustice. For "if we are not part of the solution, we are part of the problem." Many women have discovered that it is time to speak the truth . . . firmly . . . in love. As Sheila Collins points out, one of the emotions most frequently avoided in the Christian heritage is anger. It is wrongly assumed, she says, that anger is not a legitimate human feeling, especially in the face of oppression.[1] Women need to step out of the traditional passive, subordinate, and inferior roles that have been assigned to them. The title of Jean Baer's book is descriptive; in it she tells *How to Be an Assertive (Not Aggressive) Woman in Life, in Love and on the Job.* Our society has perpetuated several myths which have influenced women's self-concepts. Some of them are: (1) It is natural (and normal) for a woman to want to get married; (2) it is natural for a woman to wish to have children; (3) lack of ambition is normal and healthy in a woman; and (4) it is natural for a man to take the initiative, while it is natural for a woman to be passive.[2] The devastating effect these societal expectations have on women is helpfully discussed in Jean Baker Miller's *Toward a New Psychology of Women.*[3] Miller and others discuss the need today for women to escape the stereotypical mold which suggests they live totally for meeting the needs of others. More than ever women are learning, particularly through support groups, to depend on their own capabilities and discover authenticity through self-directed and goal-oriented living.

In light of Christ's life women can choose a life that moves toward wholeness. Women can feel free to establish their goals. They can learn to recognize their legitimate feelings and needs. Women can assertively set their life's priorities and then act on their convictions with assurance of their great value as God's children.

James Ashbrook points out that becoming a mature adult involves breaking out of the molds and oppressiveness of society.[4] For women, he suggests, it involves arising out of women's dependent, subordinate stereotype. It means a woman should define her own life and cease from being controlled by her family, her male friends, or her boss, and should stand up and fight for herself and other women "because she has learned that her problems aren't just her own."[5]

As traditional assumptions in raising children are being called into question by psychologists and sociologists, new possibilities in relationships are opening up for women. For instance, young women are participating more in sports, and, as men always have, they are learning the basics of strategy and teamwork. In general, more and more women are experiencing bonding with other women in common work.

Women in the past, however, have often been isolated from one another because it was thought that women were in competition for men. Women often were expected to achieve status only through marrying a successful man. Women are increasingly seeing the futility of not being the subject of their own lives. Parents, likewise, are increasingly helping their daughters to pursue healthier goals in life and teaching them that they have the right to choose their options for their lives.[6] Women also are becoming less threatened in becoming close to other women.

In contrast to the culture's oppressive expectations of women, Jean Baer suggests seven basic inalienable rights of women. They are: (1) the right to have rights and stand up for them; (2) the right to dignity and self-respect; (3) the right to consider your own needs; (4) the right to self-fulfillment; (5) the right to accept challenges; (6) the right to determine your own life-style; and (7) the right to change your behavior, values, and life situations.[7]

Likewise men find maturity and fulfillment by rising above the stereotypes that, as Ashbrook describes, cause men to hide feelings and cause relationships to be impersonal and objective, hiding the real self. In doing so, the chronic burdens of stress, shorter life spans, lack of insight into self and others, and difficulty in receiving love are some of the things that will be changed in men's experiences.[8]

What is it that women want from men? Jane O'Reilly brilliantly sums up several places men may begin. She says that women want stability, cooperation, and commitment in a relationship with a man. Women do not want to be supported or given an identity. While love, for men, used to be thought of as the handing over of a paycheck, women want men to give of themselves. Rather than men expecting women to do all the nurturing and working out of emotional issues, men, she suggests, are to take responsibility for their own lives and share themselves in a love which involves faith, reciprocity, honor, and commitment.[9]

Regarding the raising of young men, she says:

> I would also like my son to rise, without thinking too much about it,
> and to go into the kitchen and start making lunch if the other people in
> the house are hungry, even if some of them are women. I would hope he
> could approach the same degree of spontaneity about laundry and shopping.
> I hope he doesn't think children are interesting only after they are toilet
> trained. I hope he gets into the college he wants to attend, but if he
> doesn't, I hope he doesn't think a woman or a minority man took away
> his rightful place.[10]

It is time for men to reevaluate their view of women and ask
themselves some hard questions: Is there any part of my life where I
am treating women with less respect than men? Are all my words about
my wife (or women in general) spoken as if I thought she was better
than I (Philippians 2:3)? Does my wife have as much freedom as I do?
Am I vulnerably sharing all of myself with my life partner? Am I
sharing my thoughts, emotions, energy, time, experiences, money, and
dreams?

It is painfully late, but it will never be too late for us to let the
Holy Spirit bring about change. We need to strive toward a Christlike
giving of our selves to our marriage partners and to others. In short,
it is time for all of us to be vulnerable and risk changing our behavior
in order to grow and to help others to grow.

Liberation is not an overnight process. When you attempt to raise
the status of women, there will be times when others will act in a
hostile manner toward you. But no matter what the cost, keep in mind
that lasting and enduring liberation comes slowly. For some women
and men the slightest mention of change in the way women are viewed
will bring on a defensive and bitter reaction. But change will come.

The whole point of trying to raise someone's consciousness about
women's equality is to promote growth, not overnight change. In many
the process of change has been one which has taken years. Some have
grown from bitterness to sarcasm, but eventually to understanding.
Lasting and enduring liberation will come if it is surrounded by patience
and love. And even if it takes years for a marriage to improve, even
if it takes several years until your congregation profits from the ministry
of women leaders, all the struggle is worth it.

One of the most beautiful things happening in creation is that new
possibilities are opening up in human relationships. The traditional
dominance/submission way of relating to others is being seen as oppressive. New and liberating patterns of relating are emerging, and

these patterns are producing long overdue changes in friendships, in love, in parent-child, employer-employee, and in clergy-lay relationships. It is up to you to make your relationships with others beautiful whether it is in friendship or in marriage. Every change you make in your attitude and actions toward that end will be a new beginning that eventually brings praise to God and a joyful wholeness to yourself and others.

The new direction Jesus turned us toward two thousand years ago was only a start. For each of us, every day can be a new beginning. "Therefore, if any one is in Christ, he [or she] is a new creation; the old has passed away, behold, the new has come" (2 Corinthians 5:17).

It would have been interesting to end this book with a continuation of the short story from the preface, but that would have been too simplistic. The changes those two people would have made would not have been your own. Each of us can have new beginnings appropriate to his or her situation and varying relationships. This is the meaning of "working out your salvation with fear and trembling" (Philippians 2:12). We can apply God's Word to our own experiences and responsibilities. In that way, life as a Christ-follower can be full of new beginnings.

STUDY QUESTIONS FOR CHAPTER 7

1. List the changes in your thoughts about women in the church and society as a result of your reading.

2. On the basis of your understanding of the biblical material relating to women, what changes do you feel need to be made in the family or in the church?

3. What things might be changed in bringing up our children in order to teach them the proper relationships between women and men?

4. What will be the cost of making these changes?

5. Single people today are often feeling left out of the church programs because of the "family" orientation. Often single women feel that they are in some ways still under their father's authority until they are married, even though they have already reached adulthood. What kinds of attitudes need to be changed about single people, and what actions should be taken to change situations affecting them?

Notes

Chapter 1

[1]Mary Crawford, "Climbing the Ivy-Covered Walls: How Colleges Deny Tenure to Women," *Ms.*, vol. 7, no. 5 (November, 1978), pp. 61-63, 92-94. Recent studies show, however, that women employed as educators find more difficulty than men in obtaining advancements.

Chapter 2

[1]Merlin Stone, *When God Was a Woman* (New York: Harcourt Brace Jovanovich, Inc., Harvest Books, 1976), p. 3. This, according to Stone, is true also in Africa, Australia, and China. It should be noted, however, that the evidence that Stone presents is more suggestive than definitive.

[2]*Ibid.*, p. 9. She is also called Innin, Inanna, Nana, Nut, Anat, Anahita, Istar, Isis, Au Set, Ishara, Asherah, Ashtart, Attoret, Attar, and Hathor, dating back to cultures around 7,000 B.C.E. and even to Upper Paleolithic cultures about 25,000 B.C.E.

[3]*Ibid.*, pp. 18, 31.

[4]*Ibid.*, pp. 63, 151, 152.

[5]*Ibid.*, p. 154.

[6]The Hellenistic period began after the death of Alexander the Great in 323 B.C.E. It should be remembered, however, that those traditions existing as recently as the early third century B.C.E. were in existence for centuries prior to that time.

[7]Euripides, *Stob.* 73, 1. "Terrible is the force of the waves of the sea, terrible the rush of river and the blasts of hot fire, terrible is poverty, and terrible are a thousand other things; but none is such a terrible evil as woman. No painter could adequately represent her; no language can describe her; but if she is the creation of any of the gods, let him know that he is a very great creator of evils and a foe to mortals." Cited by James Donaldson, *Woman: Her Position and Influence in Ancient Greece and Rome, and*

Among the Early Christians (1907; reprint ed., New York: Gordon Press, 1973), p. 10. See also the excellent article on women by Albrecht Oepke, "Gunē," *Theological Dictionary of the New Testament,* ed. Gerhard Kittel, 9 vols. (Grand Rapids, Mich.: Wm. B. Eerdmans Publishing Company, 1964), vol. 1, pp. 776-789.

[8] See Hesiod's advice to men in *Works and Days,* 405-406: "Get yourself first of all a house, a woman and a working ox. Buy the woman and do not marry her. Then you can make her follow the plough if necessary." Cited by William Barclay, *The Ten Commandments for Today* (New York: Harper & Row, Publishers, Inc., 1973), p. 116.

[9] Hippolytus, 616-644. Cited in Barclay, *op. cit.,* p. 117.

[10] Donaldson, *op. cit.,* p. 61. Socrates, however, was said to enjoy frequently the intellectual skills of Aspasia. Barclay, *op. cit.,* p. 117. Plato and Aristotle envisioned commonwealths in which women would have much more freedom than the women of their time. But they still held to the common view that women were inferior to men. See also Leonard Swidler, *Women in Judaism: The Status of Women in Formative Judaism* (Metuchen, N.J.: Scarecrow Press, Inc., 1976), pp. 18-19. We should keep in mind, however, that the thoughts of Plato, Aristotle, or any other individual writer do not provide us with an understanding of the majority of the culture.

[11] Swidler, *op. cit.,* p. 5.

[12] Sarah Pomeroy, *Goddesses, Whores, Wives, and Slaves: Women in Classical Antiquity* (New York: Schocken Books, Inc., 1975), pp. 122, 124.

[13] Donaldson, *op. cit.,* p. 11. Legally, Greek women were entirely under the rule of men.

[14] Pomeroy, *op. cit.,* p. 127.

[15] *Ibid.,* p. 129. In later Roman Egypt, however, the wishes of the woman were supposedly taken into consideration.

[16] *Ibid.,* pp. 131, 137.

[17] Donaldson, *op. cit.,* pp. 31-34.

[18] Barclay, *op. cit.,* p. 119.

[19] Donaldson, *op. cit.,* p. 52.

[20] Barclay, *op. cit.,* p. 119.

[21] *Ibid.,* p. 123.

[22] *Ibid.,* p. 124.

[23] Leonard Swidler, *Women in Judaism: the Status of Women in Formative Judaism* (Metuchen, N.J.: Scarecrow Press, Inc., 1976), p. 8. Reprinted by permission. Copyright © 1976 by Leonard Swidler.

[24] By 31 B.C.E. the Romans had gained full control over what had been the Greek world. Usually the beginning of the Roman Empire is dated from the Battle of Actium in 31 B.C.E. when Augustus became the ruler of the Roman world.

[25] Will Durant, *Caesar and Christ,* The Story of Civilization, 10 vols. (New York: Simon & Schuster, Inc., 1944), vol. 3, p. 57.

[26] Donaldson, *op. cit.,* p. 87.

[27] Durant, *op. cit.,* p. 57. Also see Donaldson, *op. cit.,* p. 88. Plutarch, *Romulus* 22.3. Cited in Pomeroy, *op. cit.,* p. 154. Plutarch says that according to the regulations of Romulus, if a man divorced his wife for any other reasons than adultery, murdering the children, or making spare keys, she would be awarded half of the property, and the other half was consecrated to the goddess Ceres.

[28] Pomeroy, *op. cit.,* pp. 150-151. Upon the death of a woman's father, she was put in the custody of her nearest male relative, unless her father designated some other male in the will as her guardian. This practice continued up to the time of Diocletian, who reigned from 285-305 C.E. If a guardian withheld approval of a woman's action, she could ask a magistrate to change the decision or ask him to appoint another guardian.

[29] Donaldson, *op. cit.,* pp. 99, 108. In 215 B.C.E. a law was passed that no woman

was permitted to own more than half an ounce of gold, wear a multicolored garment, or ride a chariot within Rome or a Roman town.

[30] Pomeroy, *op. cit.*, pp. 200-223. Some cults included Fortuna Primigenia (patroness of mothers and childbirth), Fortuna Muliebris (womanly fortune), Fortuna Virilis (cult of Venus, changer of hearts), Ceres (agricultural prosperity), Tellus (mother earth), and Isis (the nature divinity of Egypt whose popularity spread throughout the Mediterranean world). One-third of the Isis devotees named in inscriptions that were found in Italy are female.

[31] Donaldson, *op. cit.*, p. 122. In response to the rise in the status of women, writers such as Juvenal responded in bitterness and mockery. Juvenal lived from 60-130 C.E. See examples of Juvenal's writings in L. Evans and W. Gifford, trans., *The Satires of Juvenal, Persius, Sulpicia, and Lucilus* (London: Bell and Daldy, 1872), pp. 46, 56, 134.

[32] Pomeroy, *op. cit.*, pp. 191, 199-202.

[33] Musonius Rufus was born around 30 C.E. Stoicism was a highly moralistic religion based on one's duty, defined by the outworking of reason. Reason itself could supposedly be seen in the working out of the natural order of the universe. Once again, however, it should be noted that we do not have access to the norms of the entire culture. We simply do not know how influential any particular writer was in his or her time.

[34] Donaldson, *op. cit.*, pp. 127, 136-137. Musonius Rufus stressed equal education for women in numbers 3, 4, and 13 of his essays. There were cases in which some Roman women devoted themselves to philosophy and literature, of which the satire of Sulpicia is an example. See also Cora E. Lutz, *The Roman Socrates* (New Haven, Conn.: Yale University Press, 1947). Also in *Yale Classical Studies*, vol. 10, pp. 3-147.

[35] Plutarch was born around 50 C.E.

[36] Lutz, *op. cit.*, pp. 3f. While Plutarch wrote of such ideas for women, he appeared unable to foresee the possible implications of full religious and social equality.

Chapter 3

[1] Merlin Stone, *When God Was a Woman* (New York: Harcourt Brace Jovanovich, Inc., Harvest Books, 1976), p. 160. Possibly Ezekiel 23:27 was a reaction to the Isis cult brought up from Egypt.

[2] *Ibid.*, p. 115.

[3] *Ibid.*, p. 161. Many, however, may find proof lacking for this.

[4] *Ibid.*, p. 162.

[5] *Ibid.*, pp. 165, 173, 174, 178.

[6] Jacob Neusner, *From Politics to Piety: The Emergence of Pharisaic Judaism* (Englewood Cliffs, N. J.: Prentice-Hall, Inc., 1973). There is a problem, however, in learning about women in Judaism. No one wrote a book on the subject then, nor was "the place of women in Judaism" even an issue at that time. Our sources on the subject are extremely limited. We do have information on women in Judaism, but interpreting and making sense of isolated facts is often difficult and is largely determined by the structure of Judaism itself. The religious leaders in Judaism were the rabbis (teachers). The most familiar sect of these rabbis known to us were the Pharisees, but they were only part of the larger number composing the rabbinical establishment. There were also sects of the Essenes, Sadducees, the Zealots, Sicarii, and temple priests.

Jacob Neusner, *Invitation to the Talmud* (New York: Harper & Row, Publishers,Inc., 1973), p. 1: Virtually all we know about women in Judaism has been learned from the writings of the rabbis. We have the wealth of historical and cultural information in the Old Testament Scriptures giving us a glimpse of Jewish life from its beginnings to the second century before the common era (B.C.E.). We have, in addition, pseudepigraphic and apocryphal writings from the second century B.C.E. and later, written after the last canonical book was written. Some of them we know as the apocrypha; these writings are included in the Roman Catholic canon but are not in the Jewish or Protestant canon. We

98   Speaking Out for Women

also have the vast collection of religious laws, wise sayings, and stories of the rabbis
included in the Talmud, which is the most influential document in the history of Judaism.

Neusner, *Invitation to the Talmud*, p. xix: The Talmud is made up of four interrelated
documents. "First, the *Mishnah*, the law code of Judah, Patriarch of the Jewish Community of Palestine in the last quarter of the second century A.D.; second, the *Tosefta*,
a corpus of supplementary traditions associated with the Mishnah; third, the *Babylonian
Talmud*, a commentary on the Mishnah and Tosefta, produced in Babylonian rabbinical
circles between the third and seventh centuries A.D.; and the fourth, the *Palestinian
Talmud*, the equivalent, produced in Palestinian rabbinical circles from the third through
the fifth centuries A.D."

Leonard Swidler, *Women in Judaism: The Status of Women in Formative Judaism*
(Metuchen, N.J.: Scarecrow Press, Inc., 1976), p. 71: The mode of Jewish religion
known as "rabbinic Judaism" encompassed an extremely narrow range of Jewish experience. The Pharisees, who were the most influential group of rabbis, numbered only
around 6,000, and even then they had no hold on either the government or the general
population. Among the religious leadership in formative Judaism were the priests, the
Pharisees (rabbis and scribes), the Essenes, and the others who dedicated their lives to
studying the Jewish oral and written laws. There were approximately 7,000 to 9,000
priests; 5,000 Pharisees; and 4,000 Essenes in Palestine at the time of Christ. See also
M. Smith, "Palestinian Judaism in the First Century," *Judaism: Its Role in Civilization*,
ed. M. Davis (New York: Harper & Row, Publishers, Inc., 1956), pp. 67-81. While the
Pharisees and other religious leaders (such as the scribes) are generally known for their
hypocrisy and legalism in the New Testament writings, they were by and large sincere
lay people, trying to live all aspects of their life-style with religious consistency.

[7] In other words, we would be irresponsible to cite a rabbi's statement and think that
it was the unanimous opinion of all Jews of that time. In fact, throughout the Talmud
there are contradictory statements, such as: "He who has no wife dwells without good,
without help, without joy, without blessing, and without atonement" (Genesis Rabbah,
18,2), and "A woman is a pitcher full of filth with its mouth full of blood, yet all run
after her" (Talmud, Shab., 152a). Cited in Swidler, *op. cit.*, pp. 72, 80.

[8] *Ibid.*, p. 17.

[9] Philo, *Flaccus*, 89; cited in Albrecht Oepke, "Gunē," *Theological Dictionary of
the New Testament*, ed. Gerhard Kittel, 9 vols. (Grand Rapids, Mich.: Wm. B. Eerdmans,
Inc., 1964), vol. 1, p. 782. The temple was in Jerusalem, and the synagogues were
located in every neighborhood. Synagogues were the teaching and worship centers for
the community.

[10] Leonard Swidler, *Women in Judaism: The Status of Women in Formative Judaism*
(Metuchen, N.J.: Scarecrow Press, Inc., 1976), p. 88.

[11] *Ibid.*, pp. 92-93. In addition, according to the writings available to us in the second
century and onward, the rabbis suggested that women should not be permitted even to
study the Scriptures. Since studying the Law was the only formal education in Judaism
and since women did not participate in this activity, women were denied education.

Jer. Sotah, 19a; Sotah 3.4; Shab. 33b; Joma. 66b; B.M. 59a, cited by Abraham
Cohen, *Everyman's Talmud* (New York: E. P. Dutton, 1949), pp. 161, 165, 179. Not
only did rabbis discourage women from studying the Torah in the later Talmudic material,
but they also plainly stated that the intellect of women was inferior to that of men. See
also Philo, *Op. Mund.* 165, cited by Oepke, *op. cit.*, p. 782. For more positive statements,
see Nedarim 4.3 and Nid. 45b, cited by Cohen, *op. cit.*, pp. 179, 161.

[12] Judith Hauptman, "Images of Women in the Talmud," *Religion and Sexism—
Images of Woman in the Jewish and Christian Tradition*, ed. Rosemary Ruether (New
York: Simon and Schuster, Inc., 1974), p. 193.

[13] Swidler, *op. cit.*, p. 104.

[14] Cohen, *op. cit.*, p. 161; Swidler, *op. cit.*, p. 114.

[15] Oepke, *op. cit.*, p. 782. Wisdom literature praises virtuous women but at the same time speaks harshly of ambitious and talkative women (Proverbs 6:24; 7:5; 9:13; 11:22; 19:13; 21:9; 25:24; 27:15; Ecclesiasticus 9:3; 19:2; 25:16f.).

[16] Hauptman, *op. cit.*, p. 185.

[17] Letha Scanzoni and Nancy Hardesty, *All We're Meant to Be* (Waco, Tex.: Word, Inc., 1974), p. 44. In ancient Israel the eldest son received a double portion (Deuteronomy 21:16-17); and when sons survived their fathers, the widow and daughters did not receive an inheritance. Only in families where there were no sons would daughters receive an estate. In one instance, Moses saw to it that the daughters of Zelophehad received their deceased father's property (Numbers 27:5-8). If, however, a man died and had no children, none of his inheritance went to his widow. Instead, it went to the nearest male relative on his father's side or to his brother.

Roland de Vaux, *Ancient Israel*, trans. John McHugh (London: Darton, Longman & Todd Ltd., 1961), pp. 54-55: Widows without children lived out their years with their own fathers or married their brothers-in-law in the custom of the levirate marriage. In later times, however, it was more common for Jewish women to receive inheritances. Women more often received inheritances in the second and third centuries C.E.

[18] Joma 43b. Cited in Cohen, *op. cit.*, p. 305. This was later confirmed by the Talmud.

[19] Swidler, *op. cit.*, pp. 115-116. The supposed reasoning for this was the incident where Sarah laughed at God's words when Abraham did not (Genesis 18:9-16). While the credibility of women improved in later Hellenistic and Roman courts, it declined in the Jewish world.

[20] Jeb. 24: "Who loves his wife as himself, honours her more than himself, leads his sons and daughters in the right path, and arranges for their marriage soon after puberty, to him the text refers, 'Thou shalt know that thy tent is in peace.'" Cited by Cohen, *op. cit.*, p. 165.

Jeb. 62b; B.M. 59a; Chul. 84b: "Honour your wife, for thereby you enrich yourself. A man should be ever careful about the honour due to his wife, because no blessing is experienced in his house except on her account . . . A man should spend less than his means on food and drink for himself, up to his means on his clothes, and above his means on honouring his wife and children, because they are dependent upon him, while he is dependent upon Him Who spake and the Universe came into being." Cited by Cohen, *op. cit.*, p. 165.

[21] Jeb. 14.1. Cited by Cohen, *op. cit.*, p. 167. Divorce was enacted by the man only. See also Swidler, *op. cit.*, p. 166. William L. Lane, *The Gospel According to Mark* (Grand Rapids, Mich.: Wm. B. Eerdmans, Inc., 1974), p. 354. Divorce proceedings were originally established under Moses to give a wife what she was entitled to: she was to be given a bill of divorce that released her from the marriage contract and affirmed her right to remarry.

[22] Cohen, *op. cit.*, p. 168. We do not know the divorce rules, nor their uniformity of administration, in the first century. Later Talmudic viewpoints from the second century onward can be observed in Mishnah: Ketuboth 7.6; Keth. vii. 6.

Keth. 7,6; Tos. Keth. 7,6; Keth. 7,7; Tos. Keth. 7,8; Keth. 72a. Cited by Swidler, *op. cit.*, pp. 158-159: Some rabbis believed, then, that a woman could be divorced without financial support if she gave her husband food that had not been tithed, had sexual intercourse with him when she was menstruating, failed to separate the priest's share of the dough, or made a vow and did not fulfill it. Some rabbis understood a woman could be divorced for going out of the house without her veil on or for even talking to another man. In addition, a woman could be divorced without the Kethubah if the husband found out that his wife had taken a vow he did not know about. An example of such a vow would be not to eat meat, drink wine, wear bright colored clothing, or weave beautiful garments for his children. See also William Barclay, *The Ten Commandments for Today* (New York: Harper & Row, Publishers, Inc., 1973), p. 116.

[23] Yeb. 14, 1. Cited by Swidler, *op. cit.*, pp. 156-157: In the second and third centuries, if a man's wife went insane, he was not to divorce her.

Cohen, *op. cit.*, p. 169: A woman could ask the court to compel her husband to give her a divorce. Grounds for such a divorce included blemishes appearing on the man, leprosy, or the man's having a repugnant occupation, such as a gatherer of dogs' dung, a copper smelter, or a tanner; explained in Barclay, *op. cit.*, p. 109. She could request action from the court when her brother-in-law refused to continue her husband's progeny through her (levirate marriage). Swidler, *op. cit.*, pp. 162-163. A woman technically could ask the courts to make her husband give the *Get* (divorce) if he failed to consummate the marriage (Keth. 13:5; Ned. 11.12) or to support the family (Keth. 77a) and when she wanted to get an extension of a vow of chastity from a court (Keth. 77a, v. 6).

Hauptman, *op. cit.*, p. 195: There was even a minimum dowry set in Ketuboth 67 and a percentage of a father's inheritance set in Ketuboth 68a.

[24] Hauptman, *op. cit.*, p. 194.

[25] Barclay, *op. cit.*, p. 97. This test mentioned in Numbers 5 is developed in the Mishnah tractate Sotah.

[26] Oepke, *op. cit.*, p. 781.

[27] Philo died about 40 C.E. He lived in Alexandria and is considered a representative of Judaism of the Diaspora.

[28] *Flaccus*, 89 (Philo's description of Jewish women in Egypt): "Their women are kept in seclusion, never even approaching the outer doors, and their maidens are confined to the inner chambers, who for modesty's sake avoided the sight of men, even of their closest relations." Cited by Swidler, *op. cit.*, p. 120.

Philo, *De specialibus legibus*, III, 169: "The women are best suited to the indoor life which never strays from the house, within which the middle door is taken by the maidens as their boundary, and the outer door by those who have reached full womanhood." Cited by Swidler, *op. cit.*, p. 120.

[29] *Ibid.*, p. 121.

[30] H. Schauss, *The Lifetime of a Jew* (New York: Union of American Hebrew Congregations, 1950), pp. 71-72. Describes the myth in our language. Cited by Sally Priesand, *Judaism and the New Woman* (New York: Behrman House, Inc., 1975), p. 4. For other interesting superstitions about women in that culture, see Cohen, *op. cit.*, p. 295, and Oepke, *op. cit.*, p. 791.

[31] Wisdom literature includes Job, Proverbs, Ecclesiastes, The Wisdom of Solomon, Ecclesiasticus, and some of the Psalms.

[32] Meg. 14a. Cited by Cohen, *op. cit.*, p. 123.

[33] Swidler, *op. cit.*, pp. 30-31. In the Song, it is the woman who initiates most of the action and has most of the dialogue.

Chapter 4

[1] Norman Perrin, *Rediscovering the Teaching of Jesus* (New York: Harper & Row, Publishers, Inc., 1967), pp. 39-49. This is a helpful discussion on how New Testament scholars attempt to arrive at a more accurate reconstruction of the life and teachings of Jesus.

[2] There was not a uniform set of laws carried out in every court in Palestine simply because these laws were based on oral traditions of the rabbis. See the previous chapter's discussion on divorce in Judaism.

[3] "For any cause," adds Matthew (Matthew 19:3); see also Luke 16:18.

[4] This incident is told in the context of Jesus' healing Jairus' daughter.

[5] In the Synoptic Gospels, Luke omits this incident, although it is possible that parts of the tradition are scattered in Luke 11:13, 37-41 and 16:21. Mark portrays the woman

as a non-Jew, and Matthew, using Mark as a source, seems to intensify this by saying she was a Canaanite. It is possible that one of Mark's concerns in this passage was to show that ministry to the Gentiles was prefigured in the life of Jesus.

6 In the healing of the centurion's servant, Jesus is said to call the faith of the soldier great (Matthew 8:5-13; Luke 7:1-10; John 4:46-54).

7 On one occasion the Sadducees put an abstract theological question to Jesus about life after death (Matthew 22:23-33; Mark 12:18-27; Luke 20:27-40). They apparently were not really interested in to whom a woman would be married in heaven because they did not believe in resurrection from the dead or an afterlife. They were just trying to make the "supposed" theory of heaven look foolish by contriving an earthly complication of a Mosaic law (Deuteronomy 25: 5f.). Jesus quickly put the question aside by pointing out that the completed and fulfilled kingdom of God will not be concerned for male-female relationships. "For in the resurrection they neither marry nor are given in marriage, but are like angels in heaven" (Matthew 22:30).

8 See similar anointing narratives in Matthew 26:6-13; Mark 14:3-9; John 12:1-8.

9 It is, however, the Gospel of John that places more attention on the awareness, or lack of it, by the disciples (John 2:22; 12:16).

10 Leonard Swidler, "Jesus Was a Feminist," *Catholic World*, vol. 212 (1970-1971), pp. 177-183. A "feminist" is defined as one who believes and acts in accordance with the presupposition that women should have rights equal to men in all aspects of life. While women's rights was not an issue in the Gospels, what emerges from the writings is a Jesus who was an individual who could be described by the twentieth-century term "feminist."

Chapter 5

1 There is some question as to whether Junias is a man's or a woman's name.

2 The Corinthian congregation had a number of other problems, some of which were party rivalries (1 Corinthians 11:18-19), drunken disorder and gluttony during Communion meals (1 Corinthians 11:20-22), and snobbery and competitiveness over spiritual gifts (1 Corinthians 12:1-14).

3 Hans Conzelmann, *1 Corinthians*, trans. J. Leitch (Philadelphia: Fortress Press, 1975), p. 182. Conzelmann sees the possibility of the passage being an interpolation but does not press it.

4 Alfred Plummer and Archibald Robertson, *A Critical and Exegetical Commentary on the First Epistle of St. Paul to the Corinthians*, The International Critical Commentary (Edinburgh: T. & T. Clark, 1911), p. 230. Plummer suggests that the women should not claim equality with the other sex by removing the veil.

5 John Calvin, *The First Epistle of Paul the Apostle to the Corinthians*, trans. John W. Fraser (Edinburgh: Oliver and Boyd, Ltd., 1960), p. 34.

6 Markus Barth, *Ephesians*, The Anchor Bible, 2 vols. (New York: Doubleday & Co., Inc., 1974), vol. 1, p. 190. Ephesians and Colossians probably are non-Pauline. Barth, however, sees Ephesians as Pauline. He suggests that there is evidence that Paul was reflecting on the medical relationship the head has with the body in light of his contemporary Greek thought forms.

7 Henry Liddell and Robert Scott, comps., *A Greek-English Lexicon*, 2 vols. (Oxford: Clarendon Press, 1925), vol. 1, p. 945.

8 Conzelmann, *op. cit.*, p. 185, n. 39.

9 Recall the water of bitterness test for adultery when the woman's experience was one of shame.

10 Linda Mercadante, *From Hierarchy to Equality, A Comparison of Past and Present Interpretations of 1 Cor. 11:2-16 in Relation to the Changing Status of Women in Society* (Vancouver, B.C.: G-M-H Books, 1978) is an excellent summary on the treatment of the passage.

[11]M. D. Hooker, "Authority on Her Head: An Examination of 1 Cor. XI.10," *New Testament Studies*, vol. 10 (1963-1964), pp. 411-416.

[12]See Genesis 2:18-23 where woman is made to be a helper but not an inferior being to man.

[13]F. F. Bruce, *One and Two Corinthians*, The New Century Bible (Greenwood, S.C.: Attic Press, Inc., 1971), p. 106.

[14]Barth, *op. cit.*, p. 184. Barth points out that in the context of 1 Corinthians 11-13, the general discussion is how all members of the body are equally dependent upon one another. *Head* for Paul is used as if it were just another equally dependent member of the body.

[15]Bruce, *op. cit.*, p. 106.

[16]Hooker, *op. cit.*, p. 412.

[17]*Ibid.*

[18]Bruce, *op. cit.*, p. 106.

[19]Hooker, *op. cit.*, p. 415.

[20]Charles K. Barrett, *A Commentary on the First Epistle to the Corinthians* (London: Adam & Charles Black, 1968), p. 255.

[21]Conzelmann, *op. cit.*, p. 246.

[22]Mercadante, *op. cit.*, p. 51. Mercadante points out that it was not until the early 1900s that scholars had agreed that women had, in fact, prayed and spoken in the early churches.

[23]The pattern for synagogue worship was to read Scripture, offer prayers, and listen to exposition.

Chapter 6

[1]Scholars debate whether or not Ephesians is Deutero-Pauline. "Paul is identified as the author of Ephesians in 1:1 (and 3:1). The earliest confirmation of this appears in Marcion's 'canon' (A.D. 140-160). There are strong reasons to question Pauline authorship, however: the frequent parallels to phrases found elsewhere in the Pauline corpus suggest quotations from Paul by another writer; the elevation of the 'holy apostles' as the founders of the church (2:20) contrasts with Paul's occasionally jaundiced view of them (2 Corinthians 11:5; 12:11); views stated here contrast with those found in Paul (cf. vv. 5f., 10 here below); and there is a vocabulary of about 100 words unique to this letter. The view is held here that the letter reflects a response to Paul's epistles. The author's identity is unknown, as also is the audience to which he was writing since the phrase 'who are at Ephesus' is lacking from 1:1 in Codex Sinaiticus and Codex Vaticanus (and thus from modern translation)." Cited in William Hordern and John Otwell, *Proclamation—Lent (Series B)* (Philadelphia: Fortress Press, 1975), p. 35.

[2]John Calvin, *The Epistles of Paul the Apostle to the Galatians, Ephesians, Philippians, and Colossians*, trans. T. H. Parker (Grand Rapids, Mich.: Wm. B. Eerdmans Publishing Company, 1965), p. 205. Calvin goes even to the point of insisting that women cannot obey Christ unless they yield obedience to their husbands.

[3]Verse 22 gets its verb from verse 21.

[4]Markus Barth, *Ephesians*, The Anchor Bible, 2 vols. (New York: Doubleday & Co., Inc., 1974), vol. 2, pp. 610-612.

[5]*Ibid.*, p. 619.

[6]These understandings of "as to the Lord" are suggested by Barth, p. 612.

[7]*Ibid.*, pp. 183-211. See also Walter Bauer, *A Greek-English Lexicon of the New Testament and Other Early Christian Literature*, trans. William F. Arndt and F. Wilbur Gingrich (Chicago: University of Chicago Press, 1957), p. 431. Also see Henry Liddell and Robert Scott, comps., *A Greek-English Lexicon*, 2 vols. (Oxford: Clarendon Press, 1925), vol. 1, p. 945.

[8]Barth, *op. cit.*, p. 186.

[9]This seems to be the case in 1 Corinthians 11, as we have discussed in this chapter.

[10]Charles K. Barrett, *A Commentary on the First Epistle to the Corinthians* (London: Adam & Charles Black, 1968), p. 248.

[11]For an interesting treatment of the New Testament portrayal of mutuality in relationships, see Virginia Mollenkott, *Women, Men, and the Bible* (Nashville: Abingdon Press, 1977).

Chapter 7

[1]See the apocryphal works, such as the martyrdom of Perpetua and Felicitas, in Montague R. James, *The Apocryphal New Testament* (Oxford: Oxford University Press, 1924). See also Edgar Hennecke, *New Testament Apocrypha*, ed. Wilhelm Schneemelcher (Philadelphia: Westminster Press, 1963).

[2]Apocryphal books are those which were written by Jews and Christians in the Patristic period and considered unreliable by the majority of the church. They are fictionalized accounts which, in some cases, were ascribed to people who could not have written them.

[3]For interesting reading in these works, consult Montague James, *op. cit.*

[4]Martin Dibelius and Hans Conzelmann, *The Pastoral Epistles*, trans. Philip Buttulph and Adela Yarbro (Philadelphia: Fortress Press, 1972), pp. 1-10. The authorship of the pastorals is highly questioned. It is generally not considered to be Pauline. Dibelius and Conzelmann list several arguments for their view that the pastorals, particularly First and Second Timothy, were not written by Paul.

[5]This concern for widows was in evidence throughout the history of Judaism as reflected in Deuteronomy 10:18; 24:19; Psalms 68:5; 146:9; Isaiah 1:23; 10:2; Jeremiah 49:11; Malachi 3:5. Jesus intensified the warning against those who exploit widows in Luke 20:46-47. See also Acts 6:1-3.

[6]Walter Bauer, *A Greek-English Lexicon of the New Testament and Other Early Christian Literature*, trans. William F. Arndt and F. Wilbur Gingrich (Chicago: University of Chicago Press, 1957), p. 350.

[7]*Ibid.*, p. 120. See also Henry Liddell and Robert Scott, comps., *A Greek-English Lexicon*, 2 vols. (Oxford: Clarendon Press, 1925), vol. 1, p. 275. See also Dibelius and Conzelmann, *op. cit.*, p. 47, n. 19, 20.

[8]Dibelius and Conzelmann, *op. cit.*, p. 47.

[9]Perhaps the writer was referring to the "weak women" in 2 Timothy 3:6-7.

[10]The writer may have believed that Eve sinned first, but the text could be understood to portray Adam standing next to Eve during the discussion; for Genesis 3:6 says that Eve gave the apple to her husband "with her" (*Jerusalem Bible*).

[11]Dibelius and Conzelmann, *op. cit.*, p. 48.

[12]James Donaldson, *Woman: Her Position and Influence in Ancient Greece and Rome and Among the Early Christians* (1907; reprint ed., New York: Gordon Press, Inc., 1973), pp. 176, 185, 258. Evidence shows that many of the customs and pronouncements lowering the status of women continued in the congregations of the first few centuries.

[13]Cited by Dorothy R. Pape, *In Search of God's Ideal Woman* (Downers Grove, Ill.: Inter-Varsity Press, 1976), p. 156.

Chapter 8

[1]Sheila Collins, *A Different Heaven and Earth* (Valley Forge: Judson Press, 1974), p. 185.

[2]Jean Baer, *How to Be an Assertive (Not Aggressive) Woman in Life, in Love, and on the Job* (New York: The New American Library, Inc., Signet, 1976), p. 13.

[3]Jean Baker Miller, *Toward a New Psychology of Women* (Boston: Beacon Press, 1976).

[4]James Ashbrook, *The Old Me and a New i* (Valley Forge: Judson Press, 1974), p. 60.

[5]*Ibid.*, p. 46.

[6]For an excellent study, see Eleanor E. Maccoby and Carol N. Jacklin, *The Psychology of Sex Differences* (Stanford, Calif.: Stanford University Press, 1974), pp. 303-374.

[7]Baer, *op. cit.*, pp. 62-63.

[8]Ashbrook, *op. cit.*, p. 61.

[9]Jane O'Reilly, "When He Won't Take Yes for an Answer," *Ms.* (February, 1979), p. 27.

[10]*Ibid.*

Bibliography

Books

Ashbrook, James, *The Old Me and a New i*. Valley Forge: Judson Press, 1974.

Baer, Jean, *How to Be an Assertive (Not Aggressive) Woman in Life, in Love, and on the Job*. New York: The New American Library, Inc., Signet, 1976.

Barclay, William, *The Ten Commandments for Today*. New York: Harper & Row, Publishers, Inc., 1974.

Barrett, Charles K., *A Commentary on the First Epistle to the Corinthians*. London: Adam & Charles Black, 1968.

Barth, Markus, *Ephesians*. The Anchor Bible. 2 vols. New York: Doubleday & Co., Inc., 1974.

Bauer, Walter, *A Greek-English Lexicon of the New Testament and Other Early Christian Literature*. Trans. William F. Arndt and F. Wilbur Gingrich. Chicago: University of Chicago Press, 1957.

Boldrey, Richard and Joyce, *Chauvinist or Feminist? Paul's View of Women*. Grand Rapids, Mich.: Baker Book House, 1976.

Bruce, F. F., ed., *One and Two Corinthians*. The New Century Bible. Greenwood, S.C.: Attic Press, Inc., 1971.

Calvin, John, *The Epistles of Paul the Apostle to the Galatians, Ephe-*

sians, Philippians, and Colossians. Trans. T. H. Parker. Grand
Rapids, Mich.: Wm. B. Eerdmans Publishing Company, 1965.
_____, *The First Epistle of Paul the Apostle to the Corinthians.*
Trans. John W. Fraser. Edinburgh: Oliver and Boyd, 1960.
Cohen, Abraham, *Everyman's Talmud.* New York: E. P. Dutton, 1949.
Collins, Sheila, *A Different Heaven and Earth.* Valley Forge: Judson
Press, 1974.
Conzelmann, Hans, *1 Corinthians.* Trans. James Leitch. Philadelphia:
Fortress Press, 1975.
Dibelius, Martin, and Conzelmann, Hans, *The Pastoral Epistles.* Trans.
James Leitch. Philadelphia: Fortress Press, 1972.
Donaldson, James. *Woman: Her Position and Influence in Ancient
Greece and Rome, and Among the Early Christians.* 1907. Reprint.
New York: Gordon Press, Inc., 1973.
Durant, Will, *Caesar and Christ.* The Story of Civilization, vol. 3.
New York: Simon & Schuster, Inc., 1944.
Epstein, Louis M., *Marriage Laws in the Bible and the Talmud.*
Cambridge, Mass.: Harvard University Press, 1942.
Evans, L., and Gifford, W., trans., *The Satires of Juvenal, Persius,
Sulpicia, and Lucilius.* London: Bell & Daldy, 1872.
Faxon, Alicia, *Women and Jesus.* New York: The Pilgrim Press, 1973.
Hennecke, Edgar, *New Testament Apocrypha.* Ed. Wilhelm Schnee-
melcher. Philadelphia: The Westminster Press, 1963.
The Holy Bible. Revised Standard Version. 2d ed. New York: Thomas
Nelson, Inc., 1971.
Hordern, William, and Otwell, John, *Proclamation—Lent (Series B.)*
Philadelphia: Fortress Press, 1975.
Hosie, Dorothea, *Jesus and Woman: Being a Study of the Four Gospels
with Special Reference to the Attitude of the Man, Jesus Christ,
Towards Woman.* London: Hodder and Stoughton Ltd., 1946.
James, Montague R., *The Apocryphal New Testament.* Oxford: Oxford
University Press, 1924.
Jewett, Paul K., *Man As Male and Female.* Grand Rapids, Mich.:
Wm. B. Eerdmans Publishing Company, 1975.
Jones, Alexander, ed. *The Jerusalem Bible.* New York: Doubleday
& Co., Inc., 1967.
Lane, William L., *The Gospel According to Mark.* Grand Rapids,
Mich.: Wm. B. Eerdmans Publishing Company, 1974.
Liddell, Henry, and Scott, Robert, comps., *A Greek-English Lexicon,*
2 vols. Oxford: Clarendon Press, 1925.

Lipman, Eugene, trans. *The Mishnah*. New York: The Viking Press, 1973.

Lutz, Cora E., *The Roman Socrates*. New Haven, Conn.: Yale University Press, 1947.

Maccoby, Eleanor E., and Jacklin, Carol N., *The Psychology of Sex Differences*. Stanford, Calif.: Stanford University Press, 1974.

Macurdy, G. H., *Hellenistic Queens: A Study of Women-Power in Macedonia, Seleucid Syria, and Ptolemaic Egypt*. The Johns Hopkins University Studies. Vol. 14. Baltimore: The Johns Hopkins University Press, 1932.

Mercadante, Linda, *From Hierarchy to Equality: A Comparison of Past and Present Interpretations of 1 Cor. 11:2-16 in Relation to the Changing Status of Women in Society*. Vancouver, B.C.: G-M-H Books, 1978.

Miller, Jean Baker, *Toward a New Psychology of Women*. Boston: Beacon Press, 1976.

Mollenkott, Virginia. *Women, Men, and the Bible*. Nashville: Abingdon Press, 1977.

Neusner, Jacob, *From Politics to Piety: The Emergence of Pharisaic Judaism*. Englewood Cliffs, N.J.. Prentice-Hall, Inc., 1973.

Pape, Dorothy, *In Search of God's Ideal Woman*. Downers Grove, Ill.: Inter-Varsity Press, 1976.

Perrin, Norman, *Rediscovering the Teaching of Jesus*. New York: Harper & Row, Publishers, Inc., 1967.

Plummer, Alfred, and Robertson, Archibald, *A Critical and Exegetical Commentary on the First Epistle of St. Paul to the Corinthians*. The International Critical Commentary. Edinburgh: T. & T. Clark, 1911.

Pomeroy, Sarah B., *Goddesses, Whores, Wives, and Slaves: Women in Classical Antiquity*. New York: Schocken Books, Inc., 1976.

Priesand, Sally, *Judaism and the New Woman*. New York: Behrman House, Inc., 1975.

Ruether, Rosemary R., ed., *Religion and Sexism—Images of Woman in the Jewish and Christian Tradition*. New York: Simon & Schuster, Inc., 1974.

Ryrie, C. C., *The Place of Women in the Church*. New York: Macmillan, Inc., 1958.

Scanzoni, Letha, and Hardesty, Nancy, *All We're Meant to Be*. Waco, Texas: Word, Inc., 1974.

Simpson, E. K., and Bruce, Frederick F., *Commentary on the Epistles to the Ephesians and the Colossians*. New International Commentary. Grand Rapids, Mich.: Wm. B. Eerdmans Publishing Company, 1958.

Starr, Lucy A., *The Bible Status of Women*. Old Tappan, N.J.: Fleming H. Revell Company, 1926.

Stendahl, Krister, *The Bible and the Role of Women*. Philadelphia: Fortress Press, 1966.

Stone, Merlin, *When God Was a Woman*. New York: Harcourt Brace Jovanovich, Inc., Harvest Books, 1976.

Swidler, Leonard, *Women in Judaism: The Status of Women in Formative Judaism*. Metuchen, N.J.: Scarecrow Press, Inc., 1976.

Williams, Donald, *The Apostle Paul and Women in the Church*. Glendale, Calif.: Regal Books, 1979.

Zinserling, Vincent, *Women in Greece and Rome*. Montclair, N.J.: Abner Schram, Ltd., 1972.

Articles

Crawford, Mary, "Climbing the Ivy-Covered Walls: How Colleges Deny Tenure to Women." *Ms.* (November, 1978), p. 61.

Culver, E. T., "The Old Testament." In *Women in the World of Religion*. New York: Doubleday & Co., Inc., 1967.

Hardy, E. R., "The Priestesses in the Greco-Roman World." *Churchman*, vol. 84 (1970), pp. 264-270.

Hommes, N. J., "Let Women Be Silent in the Church: A Message Concerning the Worship Service and the Decorum to Be Observed by Women." *Calvin Theological Journal*, vol. 4 (1969), pp. 5-22.

Hooker, M. D., "Authority on Her Head: An Examination of 1 Cor. XI.10." *New Testament Studies,* vol. 10 (1963/1964), pp. 411-416.

Hurley, James U., "Did Paul Require Veils or the Silence of Women? A Consideration of 1 Cor. 11:2-16 and 1 Cor. 14:33*b*-36." *Westminster Theological Journal,* vol. 35 (1972/1973), pp. 190-220.

Langdon-Davies, J., "Women and the Early Christian Church." In *A Short History of Women*. The Thinker's Library. London: C. A. Watts & Co., Ltd., 1938.

Morria, J. "The Status of Women in the Gospels." Appendix II to *The Lady Was a Bishop*. New York: Macmillan, Inc., 1973.

Oepke, Albrecht, "Gunē." In *Theological Dictionary of the New Testament*, edited by Gerhard Kittel. 9 vols. Grand Rapids, Mich.: Wm. B. Eerdmans Publishing Company, 1964.

O'Reilly, Jane, "When He Won't Take Yes for an Answer." *Ms.* (February, 1979), pp. 27-28.

Pagels, Elaine, "Paul and Women: A Response to Recent Discussion." *Journal of the American Academy of Religion*, vol. 42 (1974), pp. 538-549.

Ruether, Rosemary R., "Guarding the Sanctuary: Sexism and Ministry," and "Witches and Jews: The Demonic Alien in Christian Culture." In *New Woman, New Earth: Sexist Ideologies and Human Liberation*. New York: The Seabury Press, Inc., 1975.

_____, "The Sexuality of Jesus: What Do the Synoptics Say?" *Christianity and Crisis* (May, 1978), pp. 134-137.

Schlier, H., "Kephalē." In *Theological Dictionary of the New Testament*, edited by Gerhard Kittel. 9 vols. Grand Rapids, Mich.: Wm. B. Eerdmans Publishing Company, 1965.

Scroggs, Robin, "Paul and the Eschatological Woman." *Journal of the American Academy of Religion*, vol. 40 (1972), pp. 283-303.

_____, "Paul and the Eschatological Woman: Revisited." *Journal of the American Academy of Religion*, vol. 42 (1974), pp. 532-537.

_____, "Paul: Chauvinist or Liberationist?" *The Christian Century*, vol. 89 (1972), pp. 307-309.

Smith, M., "Palestinian Judaism in the First Century." In *Judaism: Its Role in Civilization*, edited by M. Davis. New York: Harper & Row, Publishers, Inc., 1956.

Snodgrass, Karen, and Hardesty, Nancy, "'Head': What Does It Mean?" *Daughters of Sarah*, vol. 2 (July, 1976), pp. 1-5.

Swidler, Leonard, "Jesus Was a Feminist." *Catholic World*, vol. 212 (1970/1971), pp. 177-183.

Thomas, W. D., "The Place of Women in the Church at Philippi." *Expository Times*, vol. 83 (1971/1972), pp. 117-120.

Weeks, N., "Of Silence and Head Covering." *Westminster Theological Journal*, vol. 35 (1972/1973), pp. 21-27.